LAW Of The SUPER SEARCHERS

The Online Secrets of TOP LEGAL RESEARCHERS

LAW of The SUPER SEARCHERS

The Online Secrets of TOP LEGAL RESEARCHERS

T.R. HALVORSON
Edited by Reva Basch

CyberAge Books

Law of the Super Searchers: The Online Secrets of Top Legal Researchers

Super Searchers, Volume II
A series edited by Reva Basch

Published by CyberAge Books, an imprint of Information Today, Inc., 143 Old Marlton Pike, Medford, New Jersey 08055.

Library of Congress Cataloging-in-Publication Data

Halvorson, T.R.
Law of the super searchers : the online secrets of top legal researchers / T.R. Halvorson ; edited by Reva Basch.
p. cm.
Includes bibliographical references and index.
ISBN 0-910965-34-X
1. Legal research--United States--Computer network resources. 2. Internet searching--United States. 3. Law librarians--United States--Interviews. I. Basch, Reva. II. Title.
KF242.A1H35 1999
025.0634--dc21 99-37318
CIP

ISBN 0-910965-34-X

Printed and bound in the United States of America

Publisher: Thomas H. Hogan, Sr.
Editor-in-Chief: John B. Bryans
Managing Editor: Janet M. Spavlik
Production Manager: M. Heide Dengler
Cover Designer: Jacqueline Walter
Book Designers: Patricia F. Kirkbride
Jeremy M. Pellegrin
Indexer: Sharon Hughes

Dedication

To Marilyn
for being my wife of valor
Proverbs 31:10
and
To Fay and Oscar
for giving me life and heritage
Deuteronomy 6:4-9

About The Super Searchers Web Page

At the Information Today Web site, you will find *The Super Searchers Web Page*, featuring links to sites mentioned in this book. We will periodically update the page, removing dead links and adding additional sites that may be useful to readers.

The Super Searchers Web Page is being made available as a bonus to readers of *Law of the Super Searchers* and other books in the Super Searchers series. To access the page, an Internet connection and Web browser are required. Go to:

www.infotoday.com/supersearchers

Table of Contents

Editor's Preface

The Super Searchers series is an attempt to convey, in their own words, a sense of how expert researchers think: how they conceptualize, plan, and carry out a research project; why they take one approach rather than another; what prompts them to select a particular source or medium; why basic skills and training are merely the foundation on which intuition, creativity and ingenuity all build.

The first two Super Searcher books, *Secrets of the Super Searchers* and *Secrets of the Super Net Searchers*, covered everything from market research, competitive intelligence and current events to intellectual property, engineering, medicine and the sciences. The multiple viewpoints represented in those volumes produced a rich and comprehensive picture, a composite portrait of the virtuoso online searcher at work. But the information world, and the tools and resources available to searchers, have expanded almost unimaginably in the last few years. In the age of the Web, any attempt to be broadly representative would end up spotty and superficial instead. How could we bring the Super Searchers up to date while preserving the scope of expertise and the wealth of detail that made the originals so useful and—if I say so myself—so fascinating to read?

John Bryans at Information Today, Inc. came up with the perfect solution: Let's go deep this time instead of broad, mining individual subject disciplines for their insights, both unique and universal. The law is an information-intensive profession. Legal research is specialized in both methodology and sources. Let's do a book on legal research, written by someone with a keen understanding of and interest in the field, and reflecting the perspectives of practitioners in a wide variety of settings. And so *Law of the Super Searchers* was born.

One of the joys of the online experience is its ability to connect people whose paths otherwise might never have crossed. I first corresponded with T.R. Halvorson electronically, on Compuserve, in 1990. We later collaborated on several research and writing projects, and eventually met face to face. He is a Renaissance man—a practicing attorney, a farmer, a researcher, a software developer, and a deep and original thinker. One random observation or idle speculation can turn a simple conversation with T.R. into the intellectual equivalent of a healthy aerobic workout. Like the Internet, this man's brain does not have an off switch.

T.R. selected his interview subjects with an eye toward both experience and eloquence. He elicited from all of them a feeling of love and respect, commensurate to his own, for the law and the practice of legal research. Every one of these interviews is a conversation in which it's clear that interviewer and interviewee both taught and learned from each other. I learned a great deal from reading this book. I'm confident that you will, too.

Reva Basch

The Sea Ranch, California

Foreword

Information has been the domain of librarians for centuries. When computers were added to librarians' tool kits, they were embraced. They gave us the ability to organize our own collections more readily. And they allowed us to search the databases of other libraries, organizations and traditional print publishers. Initially, when the commercial databases were Dialog and Westlaw, bibliographic citations, abstracts and synopses were all we had. When full text retrieval became available through Lexis-Nexis and Westlaw, it seemed miraculous at the time.

However, extensive as these digital resources were, the search protocols were awkward, and definitely hard to remember. The computers we used were slow, large and expensive. We had to dial into the databases, which was a tedious process with modems that crawled along at a 300-baud rate. Because of these reasons, the computers used for searching generally were located in, or near, the law library. And the librarian was the one who did the searching.

I first started online searching twenty years ago. As the law librarian for Aspen (which had a partnership with West at that time), I had the responsibility for doing Westlaw searches for the legal unit of the company. I also did research for other elements of Aspen, including the president's office. We did not have an account to access Dialog; therefore, I occasionally used the services of an information broker to do searches for us. I can remember being very excited about the results of a particular, expensive Dialog search. I showed a long list of citations—a very few with short abstracts—to a senior officer of the company. I was thrilled with the results. His reaction, however, was less than enthusiastic. He queried, "Where's the meat?" That was when I learned that decision-makers need information, the full information, and they need it on their terms, in a form they can use, and within their time limits.

Over the years my career as a law librarian has tracked with the changes that have evolved in electronic searching. We've gone from searching headnotes, indexes and abstracts, to full text. Our media have changed from paper, to microform, to CD-ROM, to the Internet. We used to be the intermediaries who did the searches. Then we started training our customers to do their own searches. Now the end user does the search, with little or no training, and advice only occasionally sought from the expert searcher.

He or she does the search at the desktop in the office, or at home; in a hotel room, or (if the television ads are to believed) while fly-fishing in Montana. This is convenient for the end-user, the decision-maker, as long as he or she knows what those in the information professions have learned over the years: Search engines and search protocols vary all over the board. Internet sites change, disappear and reappear. Once a source is located, can its content be trusted? Does it come from a credible source? Is it complete, timely and authentic?

The term that has been accepted for this trend is *disintermediation*. In April 1998, the American Association of Law Libraries held a two-day symposium with legal electronic information vendors and reference librarians which focused on this topic. The issues of end-user effectiveness and the technology skills of end users were discussed. It was agreed that the following technology-related skills are necessary for lawyers who conduct their own electronic legal research, whether using commercial databases, CD-ROMs or Internet sites:

Discrimination, necessary to identify reliable sources

Information literacy, necessary to understand information sources and the organization of information

Prioritization of sources, to enable the user to more efficiently and effectively select appropriate research tools

Flexibility and a willingness to continue learning, leading to a willingness to learn new skills, attend training sessions, and stay abreast of new developments

Consumer advocacy, lobbying information publishers to respond to user needs

What professional librarians and searchers bring to the table is the critical eye and mind. We ask who or what organization would logically have produced and disseminated the information sought, and we judge the results of our searches by criteria that measure the timeliness, completeness and authenticity of the information received. This book, *Law of the Super Searchers*, conveys to the reader how the contributors apply their talents and techniques to the digital research project. As one of them mentioned, research is an art. Most of it can be taught, but what sets these researchers apart from the rest is their intellectual curiosity, critical thinking skills, and desire to share with others what they have learned.

I am struck by how appropriate I find it to have a Montana attorney editing this book. The nature of law practice in this state has made digital legal information very popular. Like other rural areas, we have limited resources in our sparsely populated state. Montana attorneys have embraced online legal research because most simply do not have the luxury of walking down the block to use a law library.

The contributors to this guide are all experienced, acknowledged experts in our field. The reader will be well served to not just read the book and savor its lively interview format, but to refer to it repeatedly. By following these expert legal researchers' advice, the reader will be able to adapt to a continuously changing information environment, with evolving tools and unpredictable providers and sites.

Judith A. Meadows
Past President, American Association of Law Libraries
Director and State Law Librarian of Montana
State Law Library of Montana
215 N Sanders, Helena, MT 59620
jmeadows@state.mt.us
www.lawlibrary.state.mt.us

Acknowledgments

Had the editor for this book not been Reva Basch, most likely I would not have dared to try to write it. In 1992 I wrote a user's manual for an online system. My writing was lousy. I hired Reva to edit the draft, and she *saved* the manual. She has a way with language and with authors. She knows online. She edited the manual without two things: without seeing the online system and without error. Thank you, Reva, for your non-random act of kindness in giving me this opportunity.

I am grateful to Genie Tyburski, Diana Botluk, Roberta Shaffer, Cathie Best, Cindy Chick, Sabrina Pacifici, George Jackson, and Leigh Webber for sharing their knowledge with our readers. None of them needed to be included in this book to advance their careers. They did it to advance the profession. I am especially grateful to Genie for special assistance in the early part of this project.

I am grateful to Judy Meadows for reading the chapters and providing a comprehensive and comprehensible foreword. When I first read it, I had been so deep into working on the introductory chapter that reading her foreword was like flying to a hilltop and regaining perspective on where we came from, where we are, and where we are going.

John Bryans, Dorothy Pike, and Janet Spavlik at Information Today, Inc. are superb people to work for. They are accessible, and they take care of things promptly, efficiently, pleasantly, and ethically.

Ginnie Davis transcribed most of the interviews and kept me in good humor with witty side comments peppered throughout the transcripts. No doubt she will read every word to see whether I edited out all of them as promised.

My secretary, Jennifer Blekestad, transcribed the longest interview and helped capably with innumerable tasks both great and small.

Thank you, Stephanie Ardito, for advising me in true friendship.

Introduction

"These people are having an argument."

I had flown to Philadelphia to interview Genie Tyburski. The next day I took the train to Washington to interview Roberta Shaffer and Diana Botluk. On the train back to Philadelphia I reviewed notes of the interviews and listened to portions of the tapes. There were head-to-head contradictions. I surprised myself when the words passed softly over my lips, "These people are having an argument."

I looked out the window. Delaware was passing by. I was far from my home in Sidney, Montana. A few days earlier, I had left my solo-practice law office on the plains, all 750 square feet of it at the back of the old Sidney Drug Store building. I had come to the Mellon Bank Building on the corner of 18th and Market Streets where Genie works in the Philadelphia offices of Ballard Spahr Andrews & Ingersoll. When I stepped around the corner and the building first presented itself, my eyes played a trick on me: The scene went black and white as though I were stepping into *The Philadelphia Story*. On the elevator, I made a mistake. Instead of pressing the button for the 45th floor, I pressed the one for the 50th — and still got off in the offices of Ballard Spahr. What a place.

As the train approached Wilmington, my mind replayed images of the places where Genie, Roberta and Diana work. The Judge Kathryn J. DuFour Law Library where Diana works is bright and fresh, academia with a lilt. The very architecture of Covington & Burling's offices where Roberta works puts the library at the hub of the firm. That use of space reflects and supports the way the firm practices law. I thought, "I cannot do my research the way Ballard Spahr does because of my solo practice." Research has to fit in with my accessibility to clients. I live in a small town. Most of my client contacts are walk-ins and usually I, not my secretary, answer the phone. As my mind contrasted my setting with the settings of those I'd interviewed so far, it hit me: Their settings are different not only from mine but from one another's. "That's it. They're not having an argument," I said. The differences in the way they do things are driven by differences in their work settings. Diana's academic setting is different from that of a law firm. The structure of Covington & Burling is different from the structure of Ballard Spahr. These differences affect the way legal research is done.

This thought was borne out as I continued interviewing people. Sabrina Pacifici and Cindy Chick work closely together as publishers and editors of *Law Library Resource Xchange* (LLRX), yet they use contrasting approaches to a number of legal research tasks. Sabrina works in a team setting with an associate librarian, a legislative specialist, a reference librarian, an interlibrary loan specialist, a systems librarian, and a serials/circulation/accounting librarian. Nearly all assignments are done by team fulfillment. Cindy is the sole librarian in an office of seventy-eight attorneys. She likes coffee. Can you see why? Genie's attorneys are gravitating away from wanting information to wanting answers. George Jackson's law school faculty patrons often want comprehensive bibliographies. Catherine Best is a research lawyer and frequently carries the research all the way through to drafting reasoned memoranda, briefs, and factums. Leigh Webber does online legal research for the sake of being able to consult and teach. Roberta Shaffer is director of research information services in a firm that uses an intranet and email heavily because the attorneys so often are not in the office when they need research.

You are going to get different perspectives from a group this diverse. The diversity is so great that my thoughts turned the other way: "It's remarkable they agree on anything." If they agree on something, perhaps that means it is a verity. In these interviews, you'll find the range of opinion—from difference through consensus to unanimity—on various aspects of online legal research.

Through meeting these people, my own research has become more effective and more fun. This has happened despite the differences between my setting and any of theirs. Apparently, a difference in setting might account for *arriving* at different insights without blocking the *transferability* of the insights from setting to setting. I am convinced that online legal researchers will gain valuable insights that can be transferred to their own settings from each of the experts interviewed for this book. In fact, after editing the interviews, I wonder if most of us don't become too setting-bound. Perhaps the word for it is one we hope to side-step: narrow. Are we too narrow? Do our settings confine our thinking? If so, a dose of diversity might be the cure. The diversity represented in this book virtually guarantees that any reader will find chapters that are helpful.

The Interview Process

This book treats online legal research using the expert-interview approach pioneered by Reva Basch in *Secrets of the Super Searchers* and *Secrets of the Super Net Searchers*. My first step was to reread those works from the point of view of how one would set out to produce something like them in the realm of legal research. I made a purposeful effort to follow the genre while adapting it to the subject matter. I actually collated all the questions Reva used in both of her books and distilled them for the legal realm. I added to them from my own thoughts, from problems and solutions that arose while doing my own legal research, from a review of current literature on legal research, from attending continuing legal education seminars and from the initial interviews. Analysis without synthesis can leave gaps in the treatment of a subject, so I also soaked in the tub, effervesced in the steam room, and walked in the fields of my farm to sense the *gestalten* of the inquiry.

But, of course, the people themselves became the guides. These interviews reminded me of witness interviewing and two of its chief dangers: the danger of being under-prepared and the danger of following one's preparation too closely. You have to listen and follow up on what you are hearing. You can't let the next question on your yellow pad run over the top of something interesting the witness just said. Since these people are experts, often they can show you what you should be asking. Another analogy came to mind: how to search a database. Sometimes we have to listen to a database, to let it tell us how it wants to be searched. If that personification has validity, the approach must be valid when we are querying persons. Each interview took on its own unique character.

That led to the chief problem of editing. A searcher is a person. To understand how a person searches, one needs to understand the person. Lots of fascinating personal information had to be edited just to fit the material into the book. There was a good amount of kidding around and sport during the interviews that actually did say important things about searching. The trouble is, in humor we said those things either not efficiently enough or so efficiently that they were cryptic and hence, in either case, not edifying in print. You had to be there. Tone, affect and inflection do not always translate well onto paper. The portions of each interview included here vary from one quarter to forty percent of the whole. Maybe someday we can get all these people together on a panel and do it live.

Editing was another area in which I followed the genre. Reva described a delicate three-way balance among avoiding repetition, reiterating key points that others had made from their own perspectives, and emphasizing unique and important responses. You wouldn't see areas of unanimity or consensus unless, in editing, I allowed the experts to repeat important points. You wouldn't see valuable differences of opinion if, in editing, I allowed so much repetition that it elbowed out the differences. As the editing process went on, I had to consider even more carefully the reader and how the book as a whole was developing. Don't assume that because a particular expert is not recorded here as realizing a certain important insight mentioned by others that the expert did not possess that insight.

Legal Researchers and Other Researchers

Legal research seems to exist somewhat as a world apart. Many of the searchers Reva interviewed in her first book knew each other or at least knew of each other. Not many of the experts I interviewed or talked with for this book were familiar with that crowd, except for Barbara Quint and authors in her magazine. I wondered whether this or that consensus found by Reva in her first book would appear in the legal world as well. Some did. Some did not.

An example of a significant difference is how searchers build an online search. In Reva's book, searchers generally were careful not to over-qualify at the outset. In contrast, legal researchers often begin narrowly. Perhaps that stems from two factors. First, the legal researcher either is familiar with the topic or the database before the project comes in, or will gain familiarity in hard copy secondary sources before going online. That familiarity reduces the pitfalls of starting too narrowly. The unruliness of human communication in text can yield many false hits. Secondly, legal researchers search full text quite often, more often on the whole, I think, than those interviewed for Reva's book. That gives them a greater need to start narrowly. If they find too little information, they modify the search. Often, though not always, they do that by removing one qualifier at a time until the results start heading in the right direction.

Trends and Themes

Research requests come via every medium. They arrive in person, by telephone, by email, by hardcopy forms, by electronic forms on law firm intranets, by chicken-scratched notes, by Pony Express, carrier pigeon and telepathy. Well, two of those last three are exaggerations, but you get the idea.

Turnaround times are very rapid. Traditionally, "reference" questions could be answered quickly from one or two sources, while "research" questions required more time or more sources. Today, the demand for fast answers pressures researchers to treat most requests as reference questions even when they are complex, require the use of many sources, or call for a lot of material. Most requests are fulfilled the same day, many in a matter of minutes or hours. One reason for this is the speed made possible by electronic sources. Another reason is pressure. Hype about electronic information and the Internet causes unrealistic client expectations. Clients place those expectations on attorneys, and attorneys transmit them to librarians. Elements of the hype are that "Everything is online," "You just tap a few buttons on your computer and out comes everything" on your topic and "it's all free." It is not uncommon for an attorney to call the law firm's library with the client sitting in the attorney's office, ask for information, and wait on the telephone while the librarian searches.

Product delivered varies widely. The product might be an answer over the telephone or by email, a citation, a copy of a case or statute, copies of several documents with a simple cover sheet, a typed list of citations with a stack of books containing the cited materials, a formal response form giving the client name, file number, attorney or patron name, date of the request, date of the response, question presented or information requested, list of materials found, limitations and parameters of what was searched, further searching that could have been done, and a synopsis of what was found; or a reasoned memorandum, brief, or factum.

Informality reigns during intake of projects. There are exceptions, but in many settings there is little or no formal procedure or intake documentation. Sometimes the librarian jots down a few notes and gets to work. When the project is completed, the scrap of paper is thrown away. All of the researchers interviewed know what the reference interview is and know its purposes. Despite the level of informality, they all seek to achieve the purposes of the reference interview. Formal intake procedures seem more likely to occur where research is done by team fulfillment.

The reference interview is under strain. This is especially true when research requests come by email. Researchers report that requests sent by email often are less well-formed than when they come in person or by telephone. The writing skills exhibited in email are not high. For some reason, requests written in email are not as complete or well-formulated as requests written on paper (such as research request forms or memos), even from the same requestors. Those who submit requests by email tend to be less willing to respond to inquiries aimed at clarifying or detailing the requests. They tend not to return email inquiries and not to respond as well to telephone inquiries. Requests made in person or by telephone are better, although when requests come by telephone with clients waiting, attorneys may be less communicative. People who choose these modes of communication are more interested in providing added information that may be needed to target the research.

Researchers unanimously prefer all the information they can get right from the beginning. Longer requests make shorter research. Information that appears unimportant or tangential at first can become central in defining the true information need of the requestor. All researchers interviewed feel they can do a better job and satisfy their requestors better when the requestors are communicative and willing to engage in discussion of the request.

Continuing communication during a project is crucial. While some projects can be done straight through from request to final product, many require an iterative approach, with follow-up contacts and modifications of the research strategy. Ambiguities in the original request often do not initially appear to either the requestor or the researcher. The ambiguities are discovered only after the researcher has done some initial research. If the patron will not provide follow-up communication, the researcher must take additional time to perform the research several ways, making alternative assumptions about what the requestor really needs.

The stock strategies for approaching legal research that are taught in law schools generally are not used in practice by expert researchers. Expert researchers do not follow one or even several standard approaches. They think about the particular information being sought and approach the search in *ad hoc*, tailored ways. When researchers are less familiar with a topic and time permits, they do tend to fall back to the principles underlying stock approaches. Those principles generally call for beginning with secondary authority (treatises, law review articles, ALR annotations, loose-leaf services, and encyclopedias) in order to gain familiarity with the topic and with the terminology that might be used in formulating search queries.

Expert legal researchers distinguish areas driven by legal principles from areas that are fact-driven. In areas driven by legal principles, researchers stay in secondary sources longer and consult them in hardcopy. In fact-driven areas, researchers go online much sooner and formulate their queries with an eye to matching fact patterns between the case the law firm is handling and the cases they hope are reported online.

Expert legal researchers get into statutory law sooner than beginning or intermediate researchers do. The common law roots of Anglo-American and Anglo-Canadian jurisprudence conditions lawyers to think first of case law. A shift in legal philosophy over the years has made statutory law more important than many law school graduates realize. Researchers who came into legal research by avenues other than law school have been quicker to see how much of the law is controlled by statute. They, and other expert legal researchers who have caught on to the same realization, are more likely to search statutes first.

Checklists and pathfinders are seldom used. The librarian must *be* the pathfinder. After gaining some experience, librarians carry the path or checklist in their heads. Upon initial observation, it appears as though the librarian "just knows" where to look. Librarians tend to call what they are doing "intuition." In some law firms, a new librarian shadows a more senior librarian during an orientation period to pick up the paths. There are exceptions: Librarians in law firms sometimes create pathfinders for non-legal research, such as how to find company information on the Internet or how to find expert witnesses.

Librarians are frequently asked to "get me everything on" a certain topic. Often this happens because the requestor wishes to avoid having to think clearly about what he is asking. He might just want to get the issue off his desk and into somebody else's lap. Librarians usually respond by trying to define the realm of "everything." Another typical response is to make experienced guesses about what the requestor really needs, provide some initial information, and ask what else the requestor would like. Sometimes the information provided initially is all they really wanted. Other times, providing the initial information prompts a discussion that probably should have occurred at the outset, in which the realm of "everything" is defined and limited.

Record keeping is generally deficient. "All Greeks know what they should do, but only the Spartans do it." You will find a Spartan or two in the group who describe excellent methods of documenting what they do. For them, documentation serves more than merely historical purposes. It is part of research strategy. It enhances analysis and improves results. That is one reason for keeping records. There are two other reasons: for reference on the same project in case it comes back for supplementation or branching, and for reference in future projects. The non-Spartans all acknowledge that better records should be kept of what was searched and how. The records they keep usually are entirely useless to anyone but the person who wrote them. The way the notes are filed does not make them easily retrievable. Researchers periodically ponder whether they waste more time keeping records that might not be needed, or redoing research because they didn't have records in the instances when they might have been useful. Most researchers believe that, on balance, more time is wasted for lack of records. This problem does not arise because searchers fail to appreciate the value of records. It is a result of the burdens and prêssures of work settings that do not allow adequate record-keeping.

Budget has a significant impact on how research is done. The cost of research is an interplay between the cost of resources used and the cost of the researcher's time. While the resource cost of retrieving a hardcopy source might be less, the saving often is consumed by the cost of the researcher's time to retrieve that information. The total cost often would be less if the information were retrieved electronically. When researchers cannot convince requestors of this trade-off, significant time is wasted.

Everyone struggles with estimating the cost of a project. Requestors have a difficult time understanding that cost depends in significant part on how much information is found. Some researchers ask requestors how much information they expect will be found. Others ask how much they wish to spend in an initial phase, and then find what they can within that initial budget. The initial research gives the researcher some idea about how much more information might be available. Providing what was found in the initial phase sometimes triggers a decision to commit additional budget to the project. Another thicket in estimating is that information sources are fractured, decentralized, and unstandardized.

Researchers usually prefer to use statutory codes in hardcopy. This type of authority is arranged logically by topic and must be browsed to find related sections. Most researchers do not like to browse statutes online. They consider it inconvenient. If relevant provisions are spread across a code, it might even be infeasible; too many windows would have to be open on a computer screen. It is easier to have several codebooks open on a desktop.

For validating case law, researchers unanimously prefer online citators. Hardbound citators are approaching obsolescence except in smaller firms without online citators. Some searchers supplement searches in citators with searches in full-text case law databases.

For finding cases construing statutes and regulations, researchers clearly prefer annotated codes. Some prefer hardbound codes while others prefer online versions. The hardbound versions are easier to browse, but searchers need to consult online versions to bring the annotations current. If the cases are elusive, some searchers look for statute citations in full-text case law databases. While the online systems are improving their equivalencies to overcome variations in citation format, searchers do not rely on them. They search for pieces of the citation in proximity, leaving out the abbreviation and focusing on the numbers. If the citation has four or more digits, and particularly if it has a decimal, the full-text search can be quite effective. Still other researchers search for distinctive language from the statute in full-text case law databases.

Medium-neutral citation formats are gaining ground. "Medium-neutral" means citation formats that are independent of the medium in which court opinions are reported. Traditionally, cases are reported in various hardbound reporters and the citations refer to those reporters by volume number, name of reporter, and page number. Medium-neutral citation formats identify a court opinion without reference to any medium. For example, a traditional citation to *State v. Lafley* would include 290 Mont. 236, 976 P.2d 1001. "Mont." refers to the official *Montana Reporter*, "290" is the volume of that set of reports, and "236" is the page where the report of the court opinion begins. The same case is also reported in *West's Pacific Reports, Second Series*. "P.2d" refers to that reporter. "976" is the volume of that set of reports, and "1001" is the page in that reporter where the report of the opinion begins. Those traditional citation formats depend on the medium in which the opinion is reported to identify the opinion. The medium-neutral citation for the same case is 1998 MT 21. "MT" refers to the Montana Supreme Court by U.S. Postal Code format. "1998" means the opinion was issued in 1998. "21" means it was the twenty-first opinion issued by that court that year. The term could have been "medium-independent," but it is considered "neutral" in that it is not biased in favor of established publishers like West. Canada is ahead of the United States, but even Montana has adopted a format. This encourages alternative services on the Internet and by commercial providers like VersusLaw and LOIS.

Expert legal researchers almost never consult the documentation on how to search. They frequently consult documentation on library, file and database coverage. Some use hardcopy and others do it online. They are not reluctant to call customer service to find out whether a publication or document is online and in which database. This is of-a-piece with their careful file selection. The mistake of beginning searchers most commonly mentioned by experts is wrong file selection—they search a file that lacks coverage of the sources that should be searched. Veterans, knowing the importance of file selection, consult documentation and use customer support for this purpose more than any other.

Flat rate pricing has increased the amount of "grasshopper" searching. Researchers no longer need to try to make the first search statement perfect. They expect to modify most searches after seeing what they get in an initial search. They expect to learn terminology that will either recall or exclude records in second and subsequent iterations. The database itself becomes a guide to searching.

Expert legal researchers typically begin online searches narrowly. They use a variety of techniques to target their searches, starting with file selection. They tend to choose the narrowest file that will have everything they need. That takes a load off their query statements; they don't have to explicitly exclude masses of data that already are excluded from the database they have selected. They use field restrictors (e.g., date, citation, type of publication or author), phrases and proximity operators. If they think they have a term of art, they are likely to start by trying it. They search to see if it really is a term of art, and whether it is always used or whether alternative terms are sometimes used. When looking at records in early iterations of their search, they are alert to terms that are not what they are looking for, but which can be added to help exclude irrelevant documents.

Searchers usually look at keywords in context first. They examine the use of their search terms in context and do not assume a document is relevant simply because their search terms occurred in it. They differ on how much context they need to examine. Some find twenty-five words on either side of the search term adequate most of the time. Others increase the range. Some tend to switch between keywords in context and the full text of the document. They look for language to use in further iterations of the search, and references to other documents or sources that may contain useful information.

Searchers generally appreciate West's Key Number system. When they have a good key number, they give some edge to Westlaw over Lexis, but they recognize that some subjects are garbage cans, like "Appeal and Error" and "Constitutional Law."

Citators exist for dual purposes. Expert legal researchers use Shepard's and KeyCite not only to validate cases but as a research tool to *find* cases.

Preference for Westlaw or Lexis is mostly a matter of content on a search-by-search basis. Expert legal researchers are capable of producing very similar results for most searches on either system.

They choose one rather than the other based on the need for content that is either weaker or lacking on the other system. There is some preference for the system first learned, but that preference subsides over the years.

While searchers like Boolean search languages, they are gaining appreciation for natural language and relevance ranking. Natural language can be especially helpful when the searcher knows relatively less about a subject at the outset and consequently builds the search more broadly than usual at first. Natural language and relevance ranking help overcome the problem of too many hits when searching broad topics or using general keywords. While this applies to Westlaw, it is especially applicable in general Internet search engines like AltaVista.

CD-ROM seems to be on the way out in the United States. Online sources cover much of what is available on CD-ROM. Networking CD-ROMs never has become a plug-and-play technology. While a few searchers report stable operation of networked CD-ROMs, most report disappointment. In Canada, quite a bit of good research can be done on CD-ROM, enough that it probably is worth the effort to overcome networking obstacles.

Certain specialty online services are important in some settings. LEGI-SLATE provides legislation tracking information. PACER (Public Access to Court Electronic Records), CourtLink, and CaseStream provide case docket monitoring information. Congressional Universe is a subscription service that provides a wide variety of information by and about Congress, the *Federal Register*, the *Code of Federal Regulations*, and the *United States Code*. CDB Infotek provides access to public records information. Global Access provides corporate information databases. Dun & Bradstreet and Dow Jones Interactive are used in many law firms.

Expert legal researchers continually combat the notion that information on the Internet is free. First, much of the information is not "free" in the sense of being in the public domain under copyright laws. Secondly, while commercial and subscription database services are relative newcomers to the Internet, they are there now and constitute a significant presence. Lexis-Nexis, Westlaw, VersusLaw, LOIS, Dun & Bradstreet, Dow Jones Interactive, and Dialog, to name a few, are on the Internet or offer Internet versions of their services—and they cost money. Because of the presence of such services, statements about what can and cannot be done on the Internet need to be qualified.

Expert legal researchers take a tempered view of the "free" Internet. They are not caught up in hype. Excluding consideration of commercial subscription services on the Web like VersusLaw and LOIS, and the Web versions of Westlaw and Lexis, they identify numerous, serious deficiencies of the Internet for legal research, including:

lack of significant backfile: Case law collections, for example, seldom go back farther than 1992. A notable exception is United States Supreme Court cases.

lack of cross-file searching: Nowhere on the Internet can you search the court decisions of all fifty states or all federal circuits at once. Nowhere can you search simultaneously a selection of files like, for example, the Montana Supreme Court, the Federal District Court for the District of Montana, and the Ninth Circuit. Nowhere can you search simultaneously across state statutory codes.

disparity of file formats: Court opinions from different jurisdictions appear in different formats. Some are in hypertext markup language (HTML) while others are in ASCII or plain text, WordPerfect, rich text format (RTF), or other formats. Margins range all over the page. Reformatting for use in memoranda and briefs is more work than it should be.

mediocre document presentation: Court opinions often take minimal advantage of HTML and lack formatting such as italics in citations. Canadian court opinions are a wonderful exception. Many Canadian courts provide nicely formatted opinions and a choice of file formats.

deficient search facilities: Some sites that offer court opinions have no search facility at all. Few offer the powerful search features expert searchers need, such as field or segment searching, restrictors and proximity operators.

currency not indicated: Web pages often fail to say when they were last updated. Sites often do not document their policy or practice with regard to the currency of the information they offer.

unclear authority: Web sites very often fail to disclose the source of information, the reason the site exists, why the information is being offered, or other data needed to evaluate whether documents are authentic and complete, what biases might exist, and other factors involved in evaluating information quality. Most expert legal researchers depend on a relatively small range of sites maintained by reliable sources. By "reliable sources" they usually mean government sites and selected academic sites.

no document type searching: Generic search engines (such as AltaVista), generic catalogs (such as Yahoo!), and legal catalogs (such as FindLaw) seldom provide the ability to search by document type, such as law firm newsletters or court opinions. A notable exception is Law Runner.

too generic: Generic search tools (such as AltaVista and Yahoo!) perform poorly at retrieving legal information, except for search terms that are very specific and exclusive, such as "gentrification."

Expert legal researchers do use the "free" Internet where it shines. The Internet does excel in certain ways and certain places, including:

currency: This is the flip side of the shallow backfile deficiency. Often, information available on the Internet is more current than elsewhere.

government documents: The authority of a Web version of a government document is the same as the authority of a print version. Many government documents now exist only online. Obtaining the information from an agency without using the Internet might require time-consuming procedures such as a Freedom of Information Act request.

government agency forms: If you are in California and need a certain Hawaii tax form or a Delaware corporation form, you just might find it on the Web, nicely formatted in HTML, WordPerfect, or Portable Document Format (PDF).

federal legislation: Researchers use Thomas on the Web.

Federal Register: Researchers use GPO Access on the Web.

securities filings: The EDGAR Database of Corporate Information is on the Web.

recent cases: Recent cases from many of the federal circuits and state courts are online. Usually the collections are maintained by reliable organizations such as the courts themselves or academic institutions.

Canadian courts: The Canadian courts are far ahead of courts in the United States. Most have more cases online, superior document formats, and decent search facilities. A number of the courts authorize attorneys to present cases as they appear on their Web sites.

Canadian legislation: Several Canadian provinces have excellent sites that provide pending bills and recently enacted legislation.

international law: Lexis is stronger than Westlaw in international legal materials, but it doesn't cover everything. Sometimes the Web is the only online source of foreign law materials, and the only handy way to find it from North America.

Internet, computers, and technology: The Internet is strong on Internet-, computer-, and technology-related subjects. For example, useful documents on Internet taxation can be found on the Web.

selected legal catalogs: Most expert legal researchers do make certain uses of selected legal Web directories and catalogs. The clear favorite is FindLaw, the Yahoo! of legal information. Several of the interviewees wish FindLaw would be more discriminating and evaluative in what it includes. Others, however, note the benefits of its inclusiveness. The tension between those two perspectives is a key theme in the future development of Internet finding tools for legal information. Because of the importance and authority of federal agency sites, researchers often use the Federal Web Locator. Other useful catalogs are CataLaw, Hieros Gamos, ALSO (American Law Sources Online), and Internet Legal Resource Guide.

Law Runner: Law Runner uses the AltaVista search engine to provide targeted legal research on the Web. Searches can be restricted by domain, jurisdiction, and document type. A large set of search templates lets a searcher more easily apply the not-commonly known power features of AltaVista. Searchers also can distinguish between American law and international law.

selected academic sites: Most expert legal researchers do use selected academic sites. Cornell's Legal Information Institute is most frequently mentioned. Others they rate highly are Meta-Index for U.S. Legal Research, World Wide Web Virtual Law Library, Internet Legal Resource Guide, and JURIST: The Law Professors' Network.

listservs: Selected listservs provide invaluable collegial collaboration and information. Those frequently mentioned are LAW-LIB, NET-LAWYERS, WEB4LIB-L, LAWSRC-L, LAWLIBREF-L, GOVDOC-L, and CALL-L.

what companies say about themselves: Sometimes what a company says about itself, its officers, its products, or its services is important, independent of how reliable or unreliable it might be. In those cases, company Web sites can be extremely valuable.

opposition expert witnesses: For some reason, people will say things online that they would not say in typed correspondence or other supposedly more formal settings. The expert an adversary is using might have said some very silly, intemperate, or inconsistent things in an online discussion group or even in a document on the Web. This information can transform a cross-examination of the expert.

opposing law firms: Librarians have found research memoranda at the Web sites of opposing counsel that take a position contrary to what they are contending in current litigation.

Web sites of classes in class action suits: Classes in class action lawsuits sometimes maintain Web sites to keep the members of the class informed about the litigation. A law firm defending the class action can find valuable information at the class's site.

international news: A law firm handling an international business transaction can improve its client's negotiations with foreign news. The Web might be the only feasible way of following news from the affected country.

finding people: Legal researchers often need to obtain contact information for people. They use the various Web tools for finding telephone numbers, postal mail addresses, and email addresses.

Despite the deficiencies of the Internet for legal research, it is sometimes incompetent not to use it. "Incompetent" is a strong word, but the statement is warranted if for no other reason than that some materials relevant or indispensable to some research assignments are available only on the Internet.

Expert legal researchers are very directed in how they use the Internet. Over time they have found the sites they consider reliable, and they tend to go back to those sites directly. Many of them know URLs like we know telephone numbers. They do not need to use bookmarks or links pages. They type URLs into their browsers from memory. The sites tend to be sponsored either by government agencies or academic institutions. They consider the authority of a site indispensable; everything else is secondary. If an expert legal researcher needs to find something that is not available at a site they already know, they might use Web search tools. They prefer the specifically legal ones like FindLaw to generic ones like AltaVista and Yahoo!. They tend to, as George Jackson says, "Think bibliographically." They ask themselves who is responsible for the information or who might have an interest in it. Who would be publishing it reliably? Then, instead of looking for documents, they look for sites likely to publish reliable information on the topic. Once at such a site, they then look for documents.

***Law Library Resource Xchange (LLRX)* and *The Virtual Chase* are essential.** While these sites are not catalogs or finding tools like FindLaw, quite often articles at these sites will have done legal researchers' work for them, along the lines of the "think bibliographically" maxim. They will have surveyed the Web and found the resources one needs. They also provide qualified treatments of how to do legal research that are more valuable than many of the continuing education seminars one could attend.

Researchers must find ways to keep current with developments on the Internet. Reva Basch said, "Writing about Web research is like painting the Golden Gate Bridge. As soon as you think you've covered the subject, it's time to go back and start all over again. Every few weeks the Net seems to reinvent itself." [*Computer Life*, August 12, 1997] There is so much going on, and so much information about what is going on, that staying current can become a research specialty in itself. The experts rely on specific resources to manage this task. They use listservs, LLRX, Cornell's Big Ear, Cornell's InSITE, the ABA's Site-tation, *Internet Lawyer*, *Searcher*, *EContent* (formerly *Database*), *Database*, and *Online*.

What Makes a Good Searcher?

Often the best legal researchers got that way in library school, or as language, history, philosophy or religion majors. Being good searchers comes from their broad interest in all sorts of things. Searchers first tell me that what they like about searching is the "find." Of course, the find is rewarding. Then, as they continue talking about it, the focus shifts to the hunt. There is an internal and an external experience going on. While it overstates the separation, there is great truth in this statement: The find is for the requestor; the search is for the searcher. Good searchers like the *process* of searching. They like words, concepts, ideas, reasons, purposes, relationships, logic, puzzles, serendipity, intuition, principle, and anomaly. They like learning about new subjects as they do their jobs. Happily for them, the market pays for indulging in what, at bottom, is a personal interest.

The Role of the Legal Researcher

Legal research no longer means just research of the law. It goes beyond finding primary authority and secondary authority. It includes research in nearly all disciplines for litigation support and transaction support. Law firms are looking for information on companies, products, clients, opponents, experts, medicine, science, engineering, architecture, markets, news, technology, computers, the Internet, politics, public opinion, jury attitudes—almost any subject. In some settings you can avoid searching subjects outside the law *per se*. In many settings you cannot.

Patron attitudes toward the reference interview will change. Patrons of the reference desk always have included those who are annoyed by the reference interview. In the law firm setting, many lawyers avoid communicating directly with the library staff because of the librarian's pesky questions. Those questions expose their incompetence as information consumers, their inability to formulate what they really need. After they try searching the Internet themselves for awhile, they will come back with new appreciation for the reference interview. They will see questioning as a professional skill rather than as an idiosyncratic turn of mind. Get ready. Prepare yourself to be gracious about their previous depreciation of your role—and to be overloaded with work.

Thanks to the Web, you will have more online sources. You will be expected to retrieve relevant information from these new sources. These new sources are not tidy. The Web is not organized the way traditional online services are. Traditional online services gather related information from scattered sources into logical files, databases or libraries. For many of your searches, nobody will have done that on the Web. Say your project calls for government agency information. You might need to retrieve both federal and state information. You might need to include state information from several states. You might even need county or parish information. There is not one site where you can cover all that in a single search. You have to navigate around the Web to many sites, and perform multiple searches with different (or no) search facilities, yielding documents in different formats. The sources, the search facilities and the data formats are Balkanized and fractured. The terrain of the Web reflects the terrain of the original sources. It's great that it's "there," but you've got to know where "there" is. Your patrons think they know. They think "it's on the Internet." To them, that sounds like one place. The fact that it sounds to them like one place will set the standard of what is expected from you.

To succeed in this fractured setting, the maxim "Think bibliographically" will be more important than ever. Instead of thinking, "Which library on Lexis or which database on Westlaw has this information?" you will need to ask yourself, "Who is responsible for this information, or who has an interest in this information, which might cause them to publish it online?" You can't think of where it is gathered, because it isn't. You must think of where it came from.

Despite the already phenomenal growth of the Web, there are trends that could heighten its growth even more. Federal agencies are under a legal mandate to publish information, and the Web is the way they are choosing to publish. While there was some leveling off in the growth of the Web overall in the last two years, that has not been true of federal agency information. Those same two years saw substantial growth of federal agency information.

Another trend relates to the Year 2000 problem. A lot of government and corporate information budgets that could have gone to developing Internet resources have been diverted to dealing with Y2K. When that settles down, funds could flow back to developing the content and retrievability of Internet information from myriad government and corporate sources. Two more trends are the decline in the cost of data storage and the development of software for mounting data on the Web and making it searchable. In just the last couple of years, hard drives have become much larger and cheaper. Only a few years ago, if someone wanted to create an online service to publish information, finding and learning to use software suited to the task was a serious barrier. Today, some of the best state court Web sites are powered by off-the-shelf software. A good example is the North Dakota Supreme Court site, which is powered by Back Office. These and other trends could converge to produce a growth in Internet information relevant to legal research that might overshadow the growth we have seen already. We think we've seen an explosion of information but the next one might be the *real* explosion. There might even come a phase when librarians feel (I say feel, not think) the information world is flat. It might become so huge that no one can perceive its curvature.

Knowledge Management

In such a setting, knowledge management will be more important than ever. For a time, knowledge management in the Web world basically meant browser bookmarks. The experts interviewed in this book take differing views of bookmarking. Some emphasize the importance of each legal researcher developing his or her own extensive, organized set of bookmarks. One expert publishes his collection in the form of a Web page. Another publishes outlined pathfinders on various topics.

Others say they have outgrown the need for bookmarks, but we need to be conscious of *why* they outgrew it. They outgrew it not because they're doing less knowledge management; they are doing more. Several of them, such as Sabrina Pacifici, work in firms that have created highly developed intranets. Those intranets take knowledge management to orders of magnitude beyond browser bookmarks.

We need to practice what we preach about knowledge management. We say that this is the Information Age. We say that there is a knowledge explosion. How does one manage an explosion? The explosion is one of information. Information is what's "out there;" it's what's stored and retrievable. Knowledge is what we understand. Knowledge is "in here;" it's a trait of ourselves. Information management is one thing; knowledge management is another. The true subject of knowledge management is ourselves. We need to manage what we already know, what we have already done. We cannot waste the resource of our own experience and knowledge.

We cannot keep doing the same things over as though we had never done them before. We need to save our work, our answers, our paths, our memoranda, and our collegial pointers. We need to develop reference databases. If we can't manage ourselves, how will we manage the world?

Sabrina I. Pacifici

Team Searcher

Sabrina I. Pacifici is the director of Library and Research Services at the Washington, D.C. office of the Chicago-based law firm Sidley & Austin. Ms. Pacifici is editor and publisher of *Law Library Resource Xchange* (LLRX), a unique, free Webzine with a special focus on research, management and technology topics for legal professionals. She is the author of numerous articles and a frequent speaker at legal technology conferences on legal research and Web-related topics. *Any statements, representations, inferences or impressions are those of Sabrina I. Pacifici and do not reflect upon the practices, policies, or opinions of Sidley & Austin.*

spacific@cais.com
www.llrx.com

How did you get into legal research?

While pursuing my undergraduate and graduate degrees, I worked in academic libraries, and also worked as a research assistant to several professors. My first position in a law firm was in 1979, and I chose to stay in the legal field because of the challenging, fast-paced, varied assignments, and an environment that offered opportunities for continued professional growth.

Describe the setting where you're working now.

We have 150 attorneys in this office. Our department has an associate librarian, a legislative specialist, a reference librarian, an interlibrary loan specialist, a systems librarian, a serials/circulation/accounting librarian and me. We work on a daily basis with attorneys from the D.C. office as well as from our other stateside and international offices, supporting them in their client-related work on legal and non-legal research assignments.

What realms of the law do you research?

We undertake research assignments in every practice area of the firm, probably twenty different practice areas. Most frequently, we conduct research in regulatory, statutory, legislative, corporate and business areas, Web-related work, the Internet, energy, transportation, environment, food and drug, telecommunications, white collar crime, banking and financial services, Supreme Court litigation and appellate litigation. We not only research law *per se*, but we also conduct research for client development projects. On any given day, the division between legal and non-legal research could be anywhere from fifty/fifty to twenty/eighty.

How does a research request come to you?

Research requests come to us either in person, by telephone or by email, but predominantly in person or by telephone. It is an advantage to have the personal contact with the attorney, to more clearly identify the specific terms and issues related to their request. When a request comes in by email, it tends not to be as completely fleshed out as when it is delivered orally. We always follow up on email requests. If it is practical, we contact the attorneys directly, either in person or by telephone.

Do you have a formal intake procedure?

Yes, we do. I review all the research assignments that come in throughout the course of the day. I'm in at 7:15 in the morning, so I review all assignments that may be waiting for us, whether in email or from people who have left written requests. We have a box at the reference desk where people can drop off assignments. We have a hardcopy research request form with spaces for the name, date, client number, matter number, format in which they'd like to receive the information — indicating whether they prefer book version, online version, Web version — when they require the information, and space to write out the request. We duplicate that form on our intranet. The intranet is created, implemented and maintained by two of my librarians and me. It is available at all attorney desktops throughout the firm, and they can issue requests through it using an online version of the research form. Attorneys might write a request on a piece of paper, or call us, or simply come to us directly and say, "I need this."

What's on your intranet?

At this point, we probably have the most highly developed research-based intranet of any law firm in the United States. It is organized by practice area, legal and non-legal topics, and subtopics. In each practice area, we provide attorney bios, full-text publications that have been issued from the practice area, all the commercial services we provide related to that area, including Bureau of National Affairs [42, see Appendix A] services, CD-ROMs, Lexis [54], Westlaw [60], and CCH [47] and IHS [51] services. The practice area publications include marketing pieces, newsletters, journal articles, and law review articles. We have hundreds of links that are practice- and client-specific within each practice group area; links to all our licensed CD-ROM resources, and links to technology presentations in PowerPoint format that I have prepared for continuing legal education seminars. We've captured relevant Web links, I've annotated each one, and they are run through a Microsoft Access database. We can modify them at will, and our system also allows our attorneys to add relevant links to those we have available. If you know, as a Food and Drug Administration researcher, for example, that you are going to be using specific resources on an ongoing basis, we provide them on the intranet so you don't have to search for them. You simply click on the resource from within the intranet and go directly to it. Our intranet is search-engine driven. If you don't know what's on it, you can obtain information either through a one-word search query or through an associated relevance query with Boolean syntax. The full text of all the intranet content is searchable, including our annotations, which is extremely valuable.

We also have facilitated research using commercial database services by providing menu-driven search templates within our intranet, which are used to issue query commands to Lexis and Westlaw. Every attorney has full Internet access on his or her desktop, but we suggest they begin with the intranet because, often, we've done the work for them by providing the specific sites and information they require. The intranet offers the attorneys the option to search the in-house resources first or go directly to commercial services or the Internet. We have Web-based discussion groups. We've been working on the intranet since 1995, and it is under constant development.

How quickly do you turn around your projects?

Daily. We don't distinguish between "reference" and "research." I view all requests as research, and we typically turn around any request within the same day.

Do you conduct a formal reference interview?

We don't refer to it as a reference interview, but absolutely. The people who work with me have a tremendous amount of expertise. Their training is excellent. The majority of us have worked together for more than thirteen years. We have a comprehensive knowledge of the firm's work, of the individual attorneys and their requirements. We feel very confident talking to the attorneys to ascertain the specific requirements of their research assignments. Communication here is excellent. We talk to our partners and our associates on a regular basis. We have such a consistency of personnel, both in the library and among the attorneys, that there is a real trust and understanding between the individuals involved in the research process. They know they can simply say, "You've been tracking X, Y, and Z for me. Can you continue in this vein and add this element to the research?" We are monitoring information on a daily basis for a number of attorneys.

Do you have a role in formulating the statement of the issues to be researched?

It's up to the attorney to decide the legal elements involved in an issue. However, we certainly have a significant role in formulating the overall and specific elements of the query. If an appropriate match is not found through the research, we will continue discussing with the attorney the relevant issues involved. An attorney might phrase something in a particular way and, as a result of searching, we find that the answer lies either in a different direction or on a parallel line. There is also conversation within my department, because virtually all of our research assignments are done by team fulfillment. Often our requests are multi-tiered. There may be an online element, a hardcopy element, and an interlibrary loan element. We work cooperatively, discuss the project, assign appropriate portions of it, and come back together afterwards.

How do you choose between hardcopy and online research?

It's dependent upon whether it's a statutory question, a state question, a federal question, a regulatory question, a current question or a retrospective question. For example, we always turn to hardcopy first when we are doing statutory research. We have an excellent library that we use extensively, which includes legislative histories and associated legislative materials. The *United States Code Annotated* (USCA) and the *Code of Federal Regulations* (CFR) are often easier to use in hardcopy than online. They are a cohesive set of well-indexed and easily accessible information. If we are looking for case law, we use Lexis or Westlaw, but we would also probably turn to some of our hardcopy treatises and associated practice-related materials for background. For regulatory questions, we go online, but we often do regulatory research that pre-dates the coverage of online content, meaning pre-1979. That requires us to use hardcopy.

Are you sometimes asked to "get me everything on" a certain topic?

Yes, absolutely. It happens quite often. We use our hardcopy resources; we use indexes and directories to periodical and legal literature; we use Lexis and Westlaw, we use the Web; we use Dialog [48]; we use corporate databases to which we subscribe like Global Access [52] and *Duns Legal Search* [50]. Before doing that, we clearly define the parameters of what the attorneys are looking for. We try not to go overboard on any requests. We try to be very specific. When they say they want everything, it's generally a very narrow spectrum of "everything," such as all corporate data since 1990 relating to executive directors, annual reports and press releases. We have a very good relationship with our attorneys, so we are able to talk to them very freely and openly about what they require. We don't have any problem picking up the phone and asking them to clarify the issues involved. "Here's what I've gotten so far. Let's review it together. Is this on track? Would you like more? Would you like me to stop?" So the process is always one of communication to facilitate the final result being appropriate for the attorney's request. Without good, thorough communication, I don't think you can be a successful legal researcher.

Is there a hardcopy resource you like for which there is, as yet, no good online substitute?

Loose-leaf services and treatises. Often it is difficult to do statutory research online as well. It's difficult, for example, when you're tracing a legislative history. You need to have several books open at once. You might use the *United States Code Congressional and Administrative News* (USCCAN), *United States Code Annotated* (USCA), *United States Code Service* (USCS), and *United States Code* (USC) simultaneously. When you're doing a comprehensive project, those materials are more easily used in hardcopy.

What's your preferred method of finding cases construing language in a statute?

I'd run a search in either Lexis or Westlaw for that particular language or that citation. If we are conducting legislative research to trace the origin of statutory language, we use the *Congressional Record*, and some of the states, such as California, have excellent legislative databases on the Web. Often it is good to contact someone in the state legislative library to be absolutely, positively sure that a legislative initiative has not gone farther than the content that you've been able to find online. We also use LEGI-SLATE [53], which is the superlative online legislative tracking and monitoring system in the United States. We use it consistently throughout each day to track and monitor current federal legislation. We also maintain our own in-house database for legislative tracking, monitoring and reporting.

How much planning do you do before logging on to do legal research?

We generally don't have to plan too much. We have a conversation and we elicit information from one another regarding past experience or particular notes of interest that would help us do the research. Then we go ahead and conduct our research. The conversation often is the preparation. We're online all day, basically, all of us. We hardly ever log off. I have three computers and they are on all the time.

How often do you consult the documentation for an online service before conducting a search?

I use the hardcopy documentation, such as the Lexis and Westlaw directories of online databases. Sometimes I use the directories to locate the narrowest library or file that has what I want. Sometimes I'm looking for a specific file, a particular document, a particular journal, or a particular title. I will make sure it is on the database system before I bother to go online. I also use *Books and Periodicals Online* [93] by Nuchine Nobari and Information Today's *Fulltext Sources Online* [94].

How do you build a search?

The more specific you can be from the outset, the better. Unless you are just trolling and want to see all references to a particular case in Connecticut appellate cases, you really need to be very specific. I'm not interested in spending any more time online than is required by the project. Even though I start narrow, I still can get too many hits because there is too much information available, and because of the way online information retrieval services work. It's word association and relevancy ranking. It is difficult to put in a very complex research query and expect to obtain relevant and completely comprehensive responses from an online system. You need the human intermediary to judge whether those responses are appropriate, and often try again — unless you are just looking for a particular case, know the cite, and want to do a LEXSEE to pull it up immediately.

Research is generally a process that needs constant evaluation before you decide that you're finished. If you are looking at a case and can't discern whether it is sufficiently relevant to a particular issue, go to the book, pull it out, and read the case. Make sure it is relevant before you hand a list of search results to an attorney and ask them to waste their time looking at them. It's the attorney's judgment to make whether the case is absolutely relevant, but I'm not going to give him a stack of cases that I know are on the periphery of the issue without being very careful.

How often are you searching full-text files? How do you approach full-text searching?

I often search full text. I usually use field or segment restrictions in full text on all systems whether it's Dialog, Lexis-Nexis, Westlaw or any of the others. I think a lot of people don't use field restriction as often as it would benefit them. For those of us who began twenty or more years ago, when you *had* to use field restrictors because that's the way search engines were structured, it's easier for us to say we want a headline, a title, a name, or an opinion by a particular judge. We think about that as a normal part of our research process. If you are looking for a specific issue that you know must appear in the title of the article, then you should restrict your searching to a Title field. If you are looking for the name of a case or an individual, you should use a Name restrictor. If you know that the information probably happened or appeared sometime within the past week or month or six months, you should use a Date field. If you know you want an opinion by a specific judge, you should limit by judge in the Written By field. All those restrictors help you cull your information more carefully and insure higher relevancy.

Another important part of full-text searching is file selection. If you only want *The New York Times* [85] articles, don't go into ALLNEWS on Lexis-Nexis. Go into *The New York Times* file. If you only want newer cases, don't go into GENFED ALL. Go into NEWER.

During a search, how do you decide if you are getting the right stuff?

A word in your query can't be located willy-nilly throughout the document. You have to be committed to looking through each one of the documents, at least on a KWIC (Key Word In Context) or a VAR KWIC (Variable Key Word In Context) level, or at an abbreviated version of the document, in order to ensure that the associated language and text is appropriate to the request. I review *all* the results. I prefer VAR KWIC, because I don't think twenty-five words on either side of a search term is enough. I also toggle back and forth between VAR KWIC and FULL on many documents. I like to see the surrounding content. It might have exactly the search string that I requested, but it's in the wrong state or the wrong time period or the wrong area of law. If I print all those documents and assume that I've gotten the right answer, that's not a good thing. You can't just print it and then hand it to somebody.

I'm an extremely critical consumer. I do not expect that, as a result of my request, I will get the right answer. The right answer is the answer that will satisfy the attorney. I also look for the secondary information that appears in an article — perhaps a law review article or another type of publication — that is not highlighted as a result of my search request. That may lead me onto a further path of finding associated information that could be more relevant than the information I located originally.

If you're going to search either Lexis or Westlaw, when do you gravitate toward one or the other?

I'm a fifty/fifty user of both. I gravitate more toward Nexis for the news databases. I gravitate more toward Westlaw for the comprehensive legal periodical database, because they have the Practicing Law Institute materials as well as legal journals, law reviews, and associated bar publications. For searching case law, they are both wonderful. Westlaw allows you the advantage of using a quote around a term of art, which is awfully useful. In general, though, searching case law on the two systems is a reasonably equivalent experience.

Do you use any other electronic database services?

I use lots of specialized databases like *Duns Legal Search* and Global Access. Those are commercial databases on the Web that we pay for. LEGI-SLATE is a tremendous resource. Often we receive requests to obtain information and documents from a case still in litigation. We use a lot of dial-up systems that haven't migrated from the courts. We use PACER [57], CourtLink [45], and CaseStream [46] to monitor docketing information for cases. You obtain the docket and then you see what documents are mentioned, the date, the parties, and other information associated with it. We order the documents we select through a document delivery company rather than calling the clerks of court.

When do you use the Internet? What triggers you to say, "I need to use the Internet for this?"

Am I looking for current information only, or retrospective information? You can't find retrospective information on the Web. Is it publicly available information, government information or private information? We compare the request against database contents and coverage, both on and off the Internet, before we decide to use the Web. The Web is a great people-finder. It's great for current company and financial information, product and industry information, and current federal government information.

What is it particularly lousy at?

It's particularly lousy at comprehensive legal research!

How does the Internet fit into your overall research approach?

I go to a federal agency site, to one of the metasites supported by government agencies or university libraries, to FindLaw [6], or to one of the other major legal research databases that I know and trust. It's useful to refer to the Web, but it is not a primary research tool. We use GPO Access [12] all the time. We use Thomas [15] on a regular basis. We do use some of the federal court databases to obtain decisions, but that is not a primary means of obtaining case law. Current government documents — such as press releases, reports, GAO (Government Accounting Office) reports, information that is released by particular agencies or independent organizations in the government — are often available more quickly on the Web because that's the primary means of publication now, often the only means. We certainly refer to the Web for company, industry, people, and general factual information on a particular area.

How do you access Westlaw and Lexis? Do you use the proprietary software or do you go in through the Web?

I'm using the proprietary software. I've been beta testing Lexis and Westlaw software for about fifteen years, and I assisted both companies in beta testing their Web databases and software as well. Aside from being a beta tester, I still prefer the proprietary software because of ease of use and conditioning. I've been doing it for twenty years. I'm a power searcher. I like to be able to string together my search requests quickly without having to go through a series of menus, which wastes a power searcher's time. We built our intranet templates to facilitate power searching. All the help provided in the Web product gets in the way of an expert researcher. It's probably not in the way of someone who doesn't have a tremendous expertise and knowledge of the files, databases, and structured content of Lexis and Westlaw. I would definitely refer to it when I am on the road because it's ubiquitous. You can access it wherever you are.

What are some specific sites you use on the Web?

I use a lot of the news sites. I definitely use CNN [82], *The Washington Post* [86], *The New York Times*, the *Los Angeles Times* [84], and the *Chicago Tribune* [81] for breaking news stories. I use FindLaw as an excellent research guide for locating subject-specific information on the Web. I use GPO Access frequently for government documents. I use the Federal Web Locator [24] supported by Villanova to search federal government agencies. I use the Meta-Index for U. S. Legal Research [28] supported by Georgia State University, the World Wide Web Virtual Library [30] supported by the Indiana University School of Law Library, and the Internet Legal Resource Guide [8]. I also use Law Runner [10]—part of the ILRG site—which uses the AltaVista search engine but only queries legal documents.

That's part of the problem with generic search engines. You can't specify what kind of documents you're searching.

But you can on Law Runner, and that's what makes it so useful. I like AltaVista [61] because of the power of their search engine and the natural language query format, which works reasonably well. But I use all the search engines. I never use just one.

You mentioned AltaVista because of its power. What makes it a better search engine than others?

Everybody has a favorite and I suppose I like AltaVista because it is generally straightforward to a power researcher. I like the advanced search feature where you can use date ranges. The syntax is more like you expect when you have come from the Westlaw and Lexis world. You can effectively use quotation marks and proximity.

But all these search engines are lacking in comprehensiveness, user friendliness and content. Depending on which search engine you use, you're covering only three to thirty-four percent of the Web. That's nothing. When you search Lexis or Westlaw, you are searching the entire content, depending on which library or file you're in. You really are using the Web at your own risk.

What do you like about FindLaw?

The two attorneys who created and run it are not only experts in creating Web-based content but have a thorough understanding, as practitioners, of the types of resources that legal researchers require. They have arranged them in a logical, hierarchical fashion for easy access, they keep their links current, and it's one-stop shopping for many legal research issues. It's a directory of legal resources arranged by topics and subtopics, searchable with a search engine or using menus.

Is there a usual speech you give explaining the limitations of Internet research?

I caution people to remember that not everything is on the Web. When I last checked, there were 320 million Web pages — I'm sure there are even more now — compared with a billion pages of text on Lexis and Westlaw. The choice is obvious: You use Lexis and Westlaw for comprehensive legal research. Secondly, I mention the issue of credibility. It's "consumer beware"! Who publishes the Web site? Is it a corporate, academic, or government institution, or unfamiliar individuals or groups with an agenda or product to sell? That should alert the researcher to the validity of the content of the page. Is it a page sponsored by AT&T as opposed to an organization or a group with whom you have no familiarity? You need to be very conscious of the type of material you are accessing and whether you can critically evaluate it as valid and useful.

You need to go out of your way to use as many search engines, databases, and resources as possible. If you limit yourself to one search engine, you will be assured of failure. Because the Web is such a complex and convoluted entity, it's virtually impossible to search all the contents live, real-time, and retrospectively, as you can with a commercially maintained and annotated resource.

Much of the Web is free for a reason: the information is not as comprehensive, value-added, valid, and useful to a high-level researcher as that available on a commercial Web site. It's very difficult to look at a database on someone's Net server and say, "Oh, okay, now I have all the information I need to answer this question."

The Web is very good for lots of pieces of information, but it cannot be relied upon as a primary resource for a legal researcher, because the law is so complex. The associated information is both vertical and horizontal in its relationship.

When you tell people that there is more data on Lexis-Nexis than on the Web, do you encounter incredulity?

Yes. People don't understand that search engines use spiders and robots that go out on a regular basis, touch other people's servers, obtain information from their pages, arrange that information in a hierarchical relevancy ranking, and sort it by subject, title, or other mechanisms. They touch very few pages, and they don't search the pages on the Web live. You're searching a canned database of information taken from those pages days, weeks or months ago, if ever!

Directories are different from search engines. In a directory like Yahoo! [66], the people who design and run it decide which Web sites and pages to include in their hierarchical structure. In a search engine like AltaVista, the people who design and run it use robots that gather the information included in their index.

Either way, you are missing as much as eighty or ninety percent of what's available on servers throughout the world that might be relevant to your research.

Greg Notess, a reference librarian at Montana State University, tries to do some apples-to-apples search comparisons on the leading search engines to see how much recall we are getting. At his Web site, he publishes a chart on the overlap of hits on different search engines. According to his study, there is practically none.

Any researcher who still uses multiple search engines, as I do, knows that already. There are metasearch tools like Dogpile [62] that are supposed to translate search statements into the syntax of other search engines, submit them to those search engines, and bring back a collected set of results. I don't use them. I don't trust any system to understand exactly what I'm looking for. If what I am looking for is so simple that it could be translated, I would not need that service. I would go directly to the database and file that I knew I needed. If I needed an agency document, I'd go to the agency site. I wouldn't have to search for it.

That's not to say that the Web isn't valuable. You can get great Securities and Exchange Commission documents, stock quotes, Y2K information — all sorts of wonderful things. There is a lot of information available on the Web. A lot! It just isn't necessarily always what you want.

What would you like to see happen with information on the Web so that it would be more valuable to the legal researcher?

Servers throughout the world need to be able to have their information properly indexed in a current, comprehensive fashion through a search engine. Until that happens, the Web will not become the standard bearer for the researcher.

Have you had a search where you felt sure the information would be on the Internet but you never were able to find it?

No. I'm never particularly certain that I'm going to find exactly what I want. I hope I am, but I'm not necessarily sure, unless it was a breaking news document that I just knew was going to be there. For example, I was looking for a speech that Vice President Gore made. I was assured by numerous parties who should know that it would be on the Web, and it wasn't. They told me where, but it was not there, so I also used search engines and a variety of other tools to try to find it. We finally contacted his office and asked.

We never assume that we are going to find it. We always back it up with a phone call. Often you can contact Webmasters and ask,

"Did you put the document up?" and many of them will actually say, "Oops, I forgot" or "It will be on this afternoon." Sometimes those phone numbers are on the Web site, but more often they are not. A lot of times they are in the *Federal Yellow Book*. There's a *State Yellow Book*, a *Federal Yellow Book*, and a *Congressional Yellow Book*. They're definitely useful resources for anybody who does anything with agencies on the state or federal level.

Do you use listservs?

Daily. I'm on NET-LAWYERS [75], The TechnoLawyer Listserver [79], NETWORK2D-L [77], and LAWSRC-L [72]. Most of the time I just read. I'm often surprised at the quality and the expertise of many of the people on legal listservs and their willingness to share their experiences — good and bad — relating to technology and the law. Occasionally I answer questions posed by others. In one instance a law librarian in Japan required a piece of information that I had here in my library and all I had to do was photocopy it and fax it to her.

How is the Internet affecting the role of the legal research specialist?

It's yet another tool in our arsenal with which we have to be expert and proficient. The range of information and the resources we need to use are expanding exponentially. Many people associate the Web with instant answers and free answers; that is obviously not the case. We've been able to provide our internal user group with an effective means of utilizing the Web through our intranet. That has facilitated a more realistic usage of the Web here.

Why are you a searcher? What do you like about it?

I've been a researcher since I can remember. I was a reader and a library user beginning at a very young age. Throughout college and graduate school I was a researcher for professors. I've always had a keen interest in being able to find answers to questions, from the simple to the deep and abiding.

What do you like about online searching?

I like the relational aspect of it, the ability to relate concepts, words, and information to a greater whole. I like the hunt, the process of finding. I like the collaborative effort of working with others to achieve an answer or a set of information that will meet a certain set of requirements. I have the pleasure and privilege of working with people I have known for a long time, respect deeply, and trust implicitly. I enjoy coming to work every day because of that.

What makes a good searcher?

I think it's the love of the hunt. You have to really like the process. You have to like using a variety of resources, be they online or hardcopy. You have to be focused and relentless in your pursuit. You need to develop skills that you'll be able to use in lots of other arenas, not just in your job. You need to work in a setting where you are challenged, motivated and satisfied. You have to love words, language, information and learning. You have to be motivated to wake up each day and know there is something you can learn. As simple as it may sound, the skills of being able to read well, analyze, and juggle lots of pieces of information in relationship to one another are essential in any research field.

What can people with research requests do to help a researcher do the best job for them?

Talk to them. Don't simply assume that, because you've written a line or two in an email, your question is clear, precise, and can be answered quickly and easily. The communication issue is paramount in the research process. As a requester, you should take the time to formulate your request as completely as you possibly can, and be willing to discuss, with the individual tasked with that assignment, the elements that are required to fulfill it.

How do you know when the search is done?

The search is done when the attorney is satisfied that it's done. He has to be in communication with you. Just as communication is the heart of the beginning of a project, it is the heart of knowing when the project is finished.

Is there a downside to online legal research in a general sense?

In some ways it's an unhappy trend, because it's more difficult to process information. You process online information thirty percent slower than you process information that is written or printed. The complexity of doing legal research often requires having numerous documents open at once. If we were to eliminate books and the ability to juggle them, that would be detrimental to the process. People are using the Print key with wild abandon. They are basically reprinting hundreds of thousands of books every day because they can't read it online! It's a waste; you end up throwing it out.

Tell me about *Law Library Resource Xchange* (LLRX) [1]. How did that get started?

I had been a hardcopy publisher for a number of years. I created a publication called *PLL Perspectives* for the Private Law Libraries Group of the American Association of Law Libraries. It was a twenty-four page newsletter that I edited and desktop-published single-handedly from 1989 until 1996. I had developed my expertise as a desktop publisher and an editor, and really enjoyed it. In the summer of 1996 I decided it was a good time to move to the Web. I asked colleagues who had worked with me on the hardcopy publication if they'd like to participate in a new venture. It would be a private venture for a wider community, more collaborative, and oriented toward research and technology for the legal community. It would allow us to tap the expertise of law librarians, not only in private firms but in academia, courts and corporations; lawyers throughout the country in solo, medium-sized and large firms; information science and information technology professionals, and consultants in the legal technology field. It would bring everyone together under the umbrella of a free legal Webzine providing timely and high-quality information on topics that were being discussed on listservs, in offices and in telephone calls throughout the country.

It's a free publication; you can simply click the email subscription link on our page. You will receive an email update twice a month with an annotated description of all our new articles and their authors. The articles are searchable at the Web site. We also have an archive where all our information is stored by area, according to whether it was a feature, a department, a column, or an extra. I'm the Webmaster along with Wenling Tseng. Cindy Chick and I are the editors, publishers and owners of the site. It's a daily enterprise of maintaining contact with people, soliciting articles, and transforming the materials into hypertext markup language (HTML). We first published on November 18, 1996. Our readership has tripled since January 1998. We're fortunate to have several outstanding legal research companies like Lexis, Westlaw and LEGI-SLATE advertise on the site.

Super Searcher Secrets

► *On building a search...*The more specific you can be from the outset, the better. Unless you are just trolling and want to see all references to a particular case in Connecticut appellate cases, you really need to be very specific. I'm not interested in spending any more time online than is required by the project.

- *On field and segment restrictions in full-text searching...*I often search full text. I usually use field or segment restrictions in full text on all systems whether it's Dialog, Lexis-Nexis, Westlaw or any of the others. I think a lot of people don't use field restriction as often as it would benefit them.
- *On verifying whether hits are relevant...*A word in your query can't be located willy nilly throughout the document. You have to be committed to looking through each one of the documents, at least on a KWIC or a VAR KWIC level, or at an abbreviated version of the document, in order to ensure that the associated language and text is appropriate to the request. I review all the results.
- *On traditional versus Web versions of Westlaw and Lexis...*I like to be able to string together my search requests quickly without having to go through a series of menus, which wastes a power searcher's time. We built our intranet templates to facilitate power searching. All the help provided in the Web product gets in the way of an expert researcher.
- *On the slim coverage and lack of currency of Web directories and search engines...*Search engines touch very few pages, and they don't search the pages on the Web live. You're searching a canned database of information taken from those pages days, weeks or months ago, if ever! Directories are different from search engines. People decide which Web sites they are going to include. Either way, you are missing as much as eighty or ninety percent of what's available on servers throughout the world that might be relevant to your research.
- *On what makes a good searcher...*I think it's the love of the hunt. You have to really like the process. You have to like using a variety of resources, be they online or hardcopy. You have to be focused and relentless in your pursuit. You have to love words, language, information and learning, and be able to juggle lots of pieces of information in relationship to one another.

Cindy L. Chick

Coffee, Scratch Paper, Go!

Cindy L. Chick is the director of Library Services for the Los Angeles office of Graham & James LLP. She is co-editor and publisher of the electronic newsletter, *Law Library Resource Xchange* (LLRX). She received her master's degree in library and information science, with a specialization in law librarianship, from UCLA, and has worked as a law firm librarian for twenty years. She is a frequent speaker on topics relating to the Internet and legal research. In 1994, Ms. Chick received the SCALL (Southern California Association of Law Libraries) Rohan Award for her role in helping fellow law librarians gain access to and learn to use the Internet. She was a regular columnist covering Internet topics in *PLL Perspectives*, the American Association of Law Libraries newsletter for private firm librarians. Ms. Chick is on the editorial board for the *Information Innovator's Newsletter* published by the West Group. *Any statements, representations, inferences, or impressions are those of Cindy L. Chick and do not reflect upon the practices, policies, or opinions of Graham & James LLP.*

cchick@netcom.com
www.llrx.com

How did you get into legal research?

I went to library school straight from college, partially because I wasn't sure what else to do. At that time I wasn't aware that there was such a thing as a law library. The UCLA Graduate School of Library Science had a two-year program; the second year you were supposed to specialize in a particular kind of library. Toward the end of the first year, we had a career day and Marie Wallace, a law librarian in the Los Angeles area, was one of the panelists. I listened to Marie, and talked to her afterwards about her work environment.

I remember her saying that you have to be a self-starter. She piqued my interest in law, so my second year at library school I specialized in law librarianship and interned at the Los Angeles County Law Library. I also had a part-time job at a law firm. I've been working at law firms since I graduated, with the exception of about a year and a half when I did library consulting.

Describe the setting where you work now.

Graham & James LLP is an international law firm with about 300 lawyers in the U.S. offices. I'm the director of Library Services in the Los Angeles office, where we have about seventy-eight attorneys. I'm the only law librarian in this office. This has been my typical work environment for my entire career. I've rarely worked, even when I was starting out, with other librarians. I did have a cataloger for a few years and I really enjoyed it because I could get another point of view on research projects. I've always envied librarians who started out in larger firms, working for experienced librarians. You can learn so much that way.

Besides handling reference and research, do you facilitate the lawyers doing their own research?

Definitely. I try to get them to the right sources and working in an efficient manner. There has been a significant change over the time I've been a law librarian. Toward the beginning of my career we spent more time doing online legal research because so many of the attorneys didn't know how. Now most attorneys know how to use Lexis [54, see Appendix A] and Westlaw [60] themselves. It is becoming much more end-user oriented, which is how it should be. Now I do more non-legal research and public records research. Most of the lawyers aren't familiar with that. We do skip tracing, company research, patent searching, expert witness identification and other stuff.

How do research requests come to you?

Three ways: They can come by email, by phone or they can walk into my office. Forty to fifty percent come by email, twenty-five percent by walk-in, and twenty-five percent by phone. What can get frustrating is the number of interruptions. A simple question in email can be very convenient because it reduces the number of interruptions, and it's all written out for you. I usually pick up my email every half-hour or so. But for anything more complicated, I prefer to talk face to face, or on the phone, so I can get a little background on what information they are looking for and why. Most requests have some level of complexity and I need to talk with the attorney directly. My least favorite method is when they have their secretary, associate or paralegal make the request. It adds one more person to the chain. You don't know whether you are getting all the information. In fact, usually you are not. Most of the time, I have questions about the search that the person making the request can't answer, so I end up having to talk with the attorney anyway.

What realms of the law do you research?

We do labor, antitrust, litigation, real estate, corporate, securities, and bankruptcy and creditors' rights. In this office we have a substantial Pacific Rim practice. We sometimes do international research and sometimes do research for the Tokyo and Melbourne offices. We have a sizable intellectual property department here. Intellectual property attorneys are very library-intensive so we do quite a bit of work for them.

How quickly do you turn projects around?

I typically turn a project around the same day. Very rarely will someone say, "You've got a couple of days to do this." I am anxious to get going on everything that comes across my desk and get it back out again as soon as I can, because I don't know what the next day is going to be like.

Is there a formal intake procedure for new research requests?

No. I scribble it on a piece of paper and get to work.

What happens to that piece of paper when you're done?

That's definitely an issue; it usually gets thrown away. I'm always trying to get stuff off my desk so I can maintain some semblance of sanity. I've been trying to figure out how to handle this better. I created a reference request form last year because I do need to go back sometimes and see what I did. I am trying to use that form; it's just not a habit yet. Attorneys sometimes come back and say that they've lost the search results, and ask whether I have a copy. I try to explain that if I kept a copy of all the research I did, they wouldn't be able to see me for all the paper. If I were to start downloading everything to disk, though, it might be more reasonable to save all my research.

The question is, which method slows us down more? Using a form slows us down in the beginning, but if a project comes back, we're slowed down if we don't have it.

Exactly, and I don't know which one takes more time. I was thinking about that the other day. Somebody came back asking if I could do this research. I looked at it and thought, "I could swear I did that for her two weeks ago." But it may be quicker to just redo the research than to keep track of every request. There would be benefits, though, in keeping better track of the requests, what I've searched, and where I've searched. We could make the form electronic and enter it into a searchable database. We keep talking about knowledge management, but I'm not so sure we manage our own knowledge that well. I get frustrated when I get a request and think, "I did this six months ago but I don't remember what the answer was." I would love to do a reference database that had all the requests I've gotten, some of the answers, certain places I checked or books I used, so I could get back to that information and maybe find my answer more quickly and efficiently. We can't keep doing things over again and not saving our knowledge.

What is on that reference intake form you created?

It's pretty basic: the requestor, the date, the client matter number, the request itself, where I've checked, what databases I might search, search strategies and a section for the result. I intended it as a prototype that I could later make electronic. The results section is where I would put a particular piece of information that might be useful in the future. For example, occasionally I get asked for court statistics such as how many cases were tried in a particular court. There is a really easy source for that, and I might remember it off the top of my head, but I only get that question about every six months. That's just long enough that I might forget it. I would like to put that into the results section and pull it into a database. Another thing I'd like to pull into that reference database is answers on the law library Internet mailing lists. You get some incredibly good information there. Often I look at an answer posted to a list and think, "I'm going to need this some day. Where do I put this so I can retrieve it?"

Can you search the list archives and come up with the same result?

The archives are so spotty and huge that you can't depend on them for finding what you're looking for. Many of the law library list archives have disappeared. Sometimes they just delete older messages. I try to save some of the more important messages to my own files, but I still don't have a good method for retrieving them. Unfortunately, the archives haven't been a very good answer. I hate to see the information go off into Never-Never Land.

Do you conduct a reference interview?

Sure. The reference interview is important. Sometimes I'm rushed, and the attorney is rushed, and it goes by the wayside and later I am mad at myself for not having been more thorough. Getting requests by email can be a problem. If they are not simple, I need to talk with the attorney. Frequently they will say, "Why don't you check this place for this information," and I'll ask, "What exactly are you looking for? What information do you need? Do you actually need this book, or do you need a piece of information that's in that book that I might be able to find for you someplace else?"

Do you have a role in formulating the statement of issues to be researched?

Occasionally, in the sense that sometimes they will come with a question and I'll say, "I don't think you really need that. I think you really need this. Are you sure you should be researching in this area when maybe it's in a completely different area?" That's the extent of it. I'm not an attorney, so anything that involves interpreting the law is out of bounds.

Do you use a checklist to remind yourself of places to look?

I've started to make checklists for company information and expert witness information. We get asked that kind of thing a lot and it's easy to forget a good source. I have a paraprofessional on staff and it probably would help him, too.

Are you sometimes asked to "get me everything on" a certain topic?

All the time. People walk in and say, "Get me everything on this person," "Get me everything on this company," "Get me everything on this topic." Sometimes I ask, "Do you really want everything?" Most of the time I don't do that anymore. Instead I do certain standard searches depending on the topic. It might be a periodical search, a Nexis search, a Westlaw news search, or a public records search. I deliver the results and get feedback on whether that was adequate. They almost never really mean "everything" or, if they do, they don't really want to spend the money that getting "everything" would require.

How does budget affect your research?

Budget is a constant consideration. It depends so much on what the research is, how much money the case involves, and how much they think is worth spending on a particular project. Someone might ask, "How much is it going to cost?" and I'll say "Thirty dollars," and they'll have to think about it. Another time I'll say "$700" and they'll say, "That's fine." You also have to be very careful not to assume that they have any idea how long it might take to answer a question. Sometimes people think a question is very simple and should take you five minutes to answer. The biggest mistake I can make is to spend two hours on it, spend a lot of computer research time and have them say, "It really wasn't that important. If I had known it was going to take you that long, I would have told you not to bother." That's a bad, bad feeling.

If you're asked to estimate the cost of a project, how do you do it?

I find that very hard to do. I don't know how the consultants do it. I try to give a ballpark figure, but I always have to explain that the cost often depends on the results of the search. If someone wants a public records search on a very common name, or research on a large company for which there's a lot of information available, it's going to cost a lot more. If they give me a fairly unique name and I get a couple of hits in two different files, it's going to be very cheap.

Roughly how is your legal research time divided between hardcopy sources and online sources?

About twenty percent hardcopy and eighty percent computer.

What factors trigger the use of electronic research?

I use electronic research when I'm looking for something very specific. If it is more general and I don't have a good handle on what they are looking for, I might go to hardcopy instead, and that's usually what I suggest that they do. If it's a code-related question, the codes are often easier to use in hardcopy. The other problem with the statutes is that they never use the language you expect, so using a hardcopy index can be easier than doing a word search by computer.

Are there hardcopy resources you like for which there is, as yet, no good online substitute?

Loose-leaf services and treatises. They are available online to some extent, but I haven't found using them online to be intuitive or easy. It will be interesting to see if that changes. That is an area where the online services still have some work do to, and I expect that, especially with the Internet, they'll be focusing on maximizing the potential of secondary sources. If I'm looking for a form, I go to hardcopy that, if I'm lucky, includes a disk.

What's your preferred method of checking whether a case is still good law?

In the past we tried to hit it two ways, by doing a Shepard's negative history only and an InstaCite. Now InstaCite has been folded into KeyCite and Shepard's is pulling their citator from Westlaw, so everything is in flux. We may decide to depend solely upon KeyCite, but we're going to have to feel quite comfortable with KeyCite's completeness and currency in order to do this.

What is your preferred method for finding cases that construe a statute or an administrative regulation?

Using Westlaw and the West digests. If a statute has four or more digits, you usually can do a pretty darn good full-text search on it. If you get four digits and a decimal you're in really good shape. If there are a lot of cases, I search the digests on Westlaw and tell the requestor, "I may not get every single mention of the statute, but I'll get the cases that deal with the statute in a significant way. If you really want every mention, we're going to have to do something else, such as go to Shepard's or do a full-text search." I like to use the digests because they have pretty much standardized the format of the citation and I feel reasonably confident that I'm getting the significant cases, not just ones that are briefly mentioned.

How much planning do you do before logging on to conduct electronic legal research?

I might make some quick notes. It depends on how complex the request is. Often I don't know what the synonyms are until I get online. I put the terms in and see what comes back. Sometimes someone comes in with a specific phrase and I'll think, "I don't think that's right." I put it in and POW! — it is a term of art, and it pulls up exactly what I want. Other times a phrase sounds like it should be a term of art and you get nothing because it's a little off. In some initial searches I get the synonyms and find out how I need to continue to search. That's why I'm not doing transaction-based searching. I need to do one search after another until I get it right.

Tell me more about searching for terms of art.

When the attorneys come in with what they say is a term of art, I usually start by putting in that term of art as an exact phrase, and see if I get what they thought I would. If I don't, I use most of the terms in the same sentence to broaden it a little. I keep going broader and broader if necessary. Then I check whether the term of art we started with is the only way they ever refer to it. Sometimes I'm surprised to find that it is the term that's always used. Other times there are alternatives that I discover during the search.

If you're going to search either Lexis or Westlaw, what causes you to gravitate toward one or the other?

I'm typically a Westlaw searcher. If something is available on Westlaw, that's how I'm going to do it. If something is only available on Lexis, obviously that is where I go. I generally find Westlaw easier to use. Lexis can be more flexible when you're searching for public records. I usually do public records research on CDB Infotek [43]. But if you are searching Asian names and you're not sure which is the first name and which is the last name, you need something with more flexibility, so I'll go to Lexis where I can manipulate the terms better.

Do you use other electronic databases such as LegalTrac?

We don't use LegalTrac as often as you might think. In the old days we used the *Legal Resource Index* online and in hardcopy. Now we do more full-text searching in the law reviews. Law review articles are so huge; this little entry with a small amount of information about the article often just doesn't tell you enough. The attorneys seem to have forgotten that the indexes exist. I recently had somebody ask, "If this law review is not in full text on Westlaw, is there any way I can find whether there are relevant articles in it?" I said, "Yes. If we want to be more comprehensive, we need to search *Legal Resource Index* on Lexis or Westlaw."

My all-time favorite database is TP-ALL (Text and Periodicals) on Westlaw. I can't tell you how often I get a question — whether on a legal topic or something more basic like "what does this abbreviation mean?" — and I plug some search terms into TP-ALL, pull up a few articles, and I'm done. TP-ALL is a huge database that includes law reviews, journals, Practicing Law Institute program materials, and a number of treatises. I typically run natural language searches in TP-ALL because the database is so large and West's natural language search uses relevancy ranking.

What factors lead you to use the Internet in a particular project?

I don't use the Internet a lot for legal research *per se*. Lexis and Westlaw are so much quicker and easier to use, and so much more efficient. The coverage of most case law on the Internet is very spotty. For example, there is no free archive of California cases on the Internet that goes back any length of time. So I use the Internet more for non-legal research, especially in areas where we don't have anything on the topic at hand. Sometimes, if I'm lucky, I get some great information from the Internet. If I'm not lucky, I get a lot of junk. It's very hard to predict. You can't make definitive statements like "You can't find this kind of thing on the Internet" because there is so much there now, and you can be really surprised.

On the other hand, unless I have no other sources for the information I'm looking for, I try not to spend hours digging around on the Internet. I do use the Internet for company and product information. I also use it heavily for government information, especially agency and legislative information. I use it to find a particular government publication, especially if it is recent. There is a lot of information on the Internet that doesn't fit into neat little categories, and isn't included in the databases. Say you want to get a Hawaii tax form. Once you had to go to the library or find somebody who has CCH (Commerce Clearing House) [47] for Hawaii. Now, it's no big deal. We go straight to the Hawaii tax site, pull it off and print it. It's amazing.

When would you start with the Internet?

If it's an Internet-related question, I probably will check the Internet early on. Someone recently wanted the status of Internet taxes in different states. First I did a TP-ALL search, but I was also able to find some amazing sites on the Internet with compilations of just what we were looking for. Of course, you have to be careful. I told the attorney to keep in mind that, without knowing the source of some of these sites, we cannot count on them to be one hundred percent dependable. At least it can point us in the right direction.

I was also asked to find out how CD-ROM industry standards developed. I found time lines on the Internet that talked about the standards every step of the way. I don't know how I would have found that anyplace else. When something relates to a specific industry, and especially if that industry is computer-related, the Internet is more likely to have good information. There are a lot of simple things you can solve using only the Internet. If I want information on pending federal or California legislation, I'd certainly go to the Internet first. The Internet would also be my first choice for the quick look-up type of search, such as zip code, stock quote, currency conversion, etc.

How do you evaluate the quality of Internet information?

That's not always easy. Everybody talks about evaluating the source. Government information from, for example, the Environmental Protection Agency [19] site should be just as good as the information the EPA would send me in the mail. At a company Web site, you're only getting information they want you to know, but often that is still useful information. A fifty-state survey of laws on Internet taxation is something you have to confirm, even if you know the source. The ideal source would be an attorney who is an expert on the topic. You would have to know that he is an expert. Even then, you wouldn't necessarily take his word for it. If the source is indeterminable, you have to be very careful.

Do you search Lexis and Westlaw on the Web or via their proprietary software?

I use the proprietary software. Right now it's faster. I know that both Lexis and Westlaw are working on the speed of their Web products. I think that, eventually, they'll have all the functionality. But, right now, there is no reason for me to use the Web product at the office. When I am working from home and don't have the most recent version of the software installed, I use the Web version. When they start introducing features on the Web that aren't available on their proprietary software, we'll have to think about switching.

Where do you go on the Internet?

I'm going in a lot of different directions these days. I go to Federal Web Locator [24] to get to government agencies. If it is something that I believe is frequently asked or easily categorized, I go to metasites. I use FindLaw [6] for frequently asked questions in law. For example, they do a pretty good page on the Microsoft antitrust case. I use Yahoo! [66] for frequently asked or easily categorized questions outside the law. When I know I want a specific site and don't have an address, I go to Yahoo!. Often, though, I am looking for something that is not frequently asked or not easily categorized and I don't know where to expect to find it. I might be on a fishing expedition. In that case, I go straight to a search engine like AltaVista [61] or HotBot [64].

Is there a difference in the way you build a search on AltaVista from the way you do it on Westlaw?

AltaVista is completely different from standard term searching on Westlaw, but does have some things in common with Westlaw's natural language searching. When I'm using AltaVista I just throw in the search terms and see where it goes. I do even less planning when doing an AltaVista search than I would with Westlaw or Lexis, because sometimes the relevancy ranking pops stuff right to the top. That's when you're lucky. It doesn't always work, and then I have to be more systematic about it. But that's usually my first try, especially if it's something fairly specific. I don't have to do phrase searching or any of the usual narrowing things I do on Westlaw. It often works for company Web sites.

If you're looking for law on the Web, where do you start?

FindLaw. As the Yahoo! of the legal community, they have a good overview. They have a great list of good resources and the site is kept so current. Sometimes I do a LawCrawler [9] search. At LLRX [1] I created a list of metasites (http://www.llrx.com/sources.html). Many of the metasites are fairly good but they may not be updated quite as often, so I have not gotten into the habit of using them. For state law or international law I might go to a different metasite. It would be nice if they were more selective about what they include.

How would you describe the state of development of Internet legal resources?

A lot of the free sites are still immature. It's going to take some time for them to develop.They're rarely going to be my only source for legal research because the coverage is so spotty and the retrieval tools have problems. Say you want just a little information to get you oriented on a topic and you believe a law firm has written a client article that would do that for you. Even in LawCrawler, you can't say, "I only want to search the client newsletter portion of these sites," for example. That's the problem I have most often; I'm looking for a substantive article but I end up with somebody's bio that says they do work in this area. I'm not going to spend a lot of time messing around with the Internet, because it's not free if it takes you an hour and a half to do it and you could do it on Westlaw or Lexis in three minutes. Hopefully, that's going to improve with XML and other ways of indexing documents on the Internet.

We could dream that someone would provide lots of primary legal authority and render it searchable with a wonderful index and search engine for free.

The question is whether advertising can support that kind of model. So far it doesn't look like it, which is why you have VersusLaw [59] and LOIS [55] providing databases for a fee. Perhaps that's the direction things are going to go.

Do you use listservs or newsgroups?

I'll admit it. I am a listserv addict. I'm on LAW-LIB [70], of course, and PRIVATELAWLIB-L [78], NET-LAWYERS [75], and The TechnoLawyer Listserver [79]. That doesn't count the dog-related lists I'm on at home. But I've cut back recently because I was getting overwhelmed, and I don't have really good filtering capability with the Internet account I am using primarily for listservs. At home I also subscribe to NETTRAIN [76] and WEB4LIB [80]. I can filter those, and I don't always get a chance to read them. People get jaded about listservs and say, "It's all people asking for inter-library loan now." In some respects, it's not as exciting as it was in the beginning. But it still gives you that ability to find the right person who might have the information you need.

Can you give me an example where a listserv saved your bacon?

There have been a lot of instances when it has saved a lot of people's bacon. For example, several years ago, one of the attorneys wanted to get a copy of an out-of-print book. It was forty years old but he said it was the bible on an aspect of anti-trust law. I thought, "How in the world am I going to find this thing? Who's going to want to sell it?" I put up a message on LAW-LIB asking if anybody had a copy they wanted to sell. Nobody did, but I got one response from a librarian at the law school where the author had been a faculty member. The author was retired and the librarian said, "I've got his address and phone number. You can contact him to see if he has any copies left." I contacted him. He had one copy of the book left, and he sold it to me.

How do you keep current with new legal resources coming onto the Internet?

At Graham & James the librarians have collaborated on our own Web page. If I think something is going to be useful, we put it there. Being on the listservs helps. Cornell has a service called InSITE [25] that gathers new sites from a number of listservs and creates an annotated listing that is accessible several ways, including periodic notice by email. The ABA has something called Site-tation [32]. At LLRX we do "Links in the News," which is about new resources. I do read *The Internet Lawyer* [83] and magazines like *Database* [87], *Online* [89], and *Searcher* [90]. There's really way too much to keep track of. When I need something specific, I go looking for it, maybe at the metasites, hoping that somebody has linked to what I need.

Have you ever looked for something you felt sure had to be on the Web but you never were able to find it?

All the time. One of the attorneys wanted to get information on a brokerage house and he was sure it was there. I searched and searched and searched because I did not want to go back and tell him I couldn't find it. But I couldn't. A couple of days later, sure enough, he came down to the library with the URL. I looked at it and thought, "Why in the world was I not able to find it?" When I looked at the site I understood the problem: The company name did not appear in the text. It appeared in the graphics. The search engines index text in the *form* of text but do not index what appears to our eyes as text but is actually a graphic. Can you believe they never mentioned the name of their company anywhere else on the site! I felt a lot better because it really wasn't bad searching on my part but bad design on theirs.

How do you feel about cases that are reported as imposing a legal duty to search the Internet?

It's a little scary. I read your article ["Searcher Responsibility for Quality in the Web World," *Searcher*, vol. 6, no. 9, p. 12, October 1998; www.infotoday.com/searcher/oct/halvorson.htm], and you hit exactly on the problems that would concern researchers. Too seldom will the right resource be that obvious. It's truly not so easy to find some of what those cases consider "easily accessible." Even something you've stumbled upon before might not be that easy to find again. There is so much serendipity involved with the Internet. You're going from spot to spot and hit the stuff, but sometimes you don't get there and the search sites don't help you. There are so many different ways you can go at any particular research project. Suppose you need to start with a search engine. Which search engine do you start with? What search terms do you use? Do you start at a metasite? Which metasite do you use? Do you use Yahoo!? Maybe if you use Magellan you'd get there, but you wouldn't if you use Yahoo!. I don't know. Maybe a good criterion to measure a legal duty is whether it's cataloged at Yahoo!.

Why does it matter whether you start with Yahoo! or AltaVista? Aren't they all search engines?

First, no search engine searches every site on the Web. None of them hit everything. In the presentation I give when I do basic Internet training, I explain that the Internet is not one source. It is a huge network of networks with millions of individual sources. At any point in time there might be a computer on that network that is not working. If it is not working, you won't find the information that's on it. It might work the next day, and the next person who comes along *will* find it. It's not like dialing into the big computer in Eagan, Minnesota [the home of Westlaw] where you have a bunch of people running around trying to make sure everything works all the time because, if it doesn't, they lose money. The Internet is a different kind of resource; if something is down or the search engine is not working properly, you may not find what you're looking for. Not only that, a search engine is not a live search. It's not searching the Internet as it exists today. It is searching an index of the Internet as it existed at some time in the past. Depending on the search engine, that time might be three days ago or two weeks ago. AltaVista is supposed to be fairly current but a lot of content is not indexed there.

You were talking about serendipity, how you might find something one day and not another. Is it all just chaos and luck, or are you picking up a few intuitions or tips you can pass along?

Some days it does feel like it's all just luck. I did a search last week for someone in our Palo Alto office. Their librarian was out sick. The librarian came back the next day and called me so we could compare notes on what I'd already done. She wondered if she should search the Internet since I already had. I told her she might as well, because she might find something completely different.

The people who have the hardest time with the search engines are those who approach them as if they were using Lexis or Westlaw. To some extent you have to be a lazy searcher and let the relevancy ranking do what it's supposed to do. You see people going into the search engines and doing these elaborate searches. That's probably one of the biggest mistakes. Relevancy ranking is incredibly important. I like natural language searching, though I know a lot of legal researchers don't care for it. It was a fairly easy transition for me from Boolean searching, whereas some people have a hard time not retaining complete control over the search. I think the same way about natural language searching on Lexis or Westlaw. I use Boolean if a natural language search doesn't work. But so often it really *can* work, especially if you have a subject that's broad and not very detailed. I probably use natural language fifty percent of the time. If you don't take advantage of relevancy ranking, you have to weed through such an enormous number of responses that it's almost useless.

You're listening to the database. You're letting it tell you how it wants to be searched. Westlaw and Lexis are that way, and the Internet is more so. Jump on, do something, look at the reasonable pages, notice their characteristics, and let that inform the modifications of the search.

Exactly. That's what worked with the search I mentioned about CD-ROM industry standards. I did a fairly general search, got a page that was somewhat related, but not quite what I was looking for, but it used a certain term. When I added that term, it narrowed my results to only things that dealt with the CD-ROM *industry*. The term wasn't even relevant to what I was looking for, but by looking at that page, I saw an indirect way of filtering out a lot of irrelevant stuff.

Despite the problems of searching the Web, you can find things that might not be available anywhere else. Then it becomes tremendously valuable, even indispensable. Do you have some examples of that?

I was searching for the fair trade law of Taiwan, in English, and wasn't having the best of luck. A quick search on the Internet and there it was. The source was unclear, so I located another, more authoritative, copy at another law library, but at least the attorney had something to work from while waiting for that document to be delivered. In another instance, I needed to locate a conference called the uTAS '96 Conference. I searched all the standard sources. Complicating matters was the fact that the u in uTAS is actually a symbol for micro (μ, mu). How do you search on that? I tried several variations of the name of the conference and the title of the article in the appropriate Dialog [48] databases, but nothing came up. I couldn't locate it in RLIN [99] or OCLC [98] either, so things seemed hopeless. But, before giving up, I searched the Internet. Right there in my search results was a press release about the conference, held each year in Basel, Switzerland. The article included a contact name and a more complete name for the conference, as well as an alternate title I hadn't seen before, ilmac 96. I've emailed the contact, and I did an additional search that located one copy of the conference material at the British Library. I've placed an order for the article and, though I still don't have it in hand, now I have high hopes!

How is the Internet affecting the role of legal research specialists?

It is expanding our resources tremendously. It has given us access to data we never had before, or data we would have found only with much more effort. It's making our lives more complicated, but more fun, too. When you find what you want, it's amazing. It's expanding our options for delivering information to our clients or users.

What is it about searching that you like? Why are you a searcher?

Sometimes it's like trying to put together the pieces of a puzzle, compiling parts from different databases to get your answer. That's fun. Somebody comes in with a question in an area that you know nothing about. By the time you're through, you have an idea what's going on in that area. That byproduct is rewarding. You're constantly learning how to search better.

Tell me about *Law Library Resource Xchange* (LLRX). How did that get started? Why did you do it? How did you do it?

Sabrina Pacifici approached me a couple of years ago and was interested in starting some kind of publication. As we talked about it, we agreed the Web was the only way to go. It eliminated a lot of the drudge work involved in putting together a publication, and opened up a lot of possibilities for things you couldn't do with a hardcopy publication. When you are able to link to additional information, it enhances the content incredibly. I just couldn't resist.

Super Searcher Secrets

- *On knowledge management...*We keep talking about knowledge management, but I'm not so sure we manage our own knowledge that well. I get frustrated when I get a request and think, "I did this six months ago but I don't remember what the answer was." I would love to do a reference database that had all the requests I've gotten. We can't keep doing things over again and not saving our knowledge.

- *On what triggers computer research...*I use electronic research when I'm looking for something very specific. Computers usually work well for specific questions. If it is more general, and I don't have a good handle on what they are looking for, I might go to hardcopy instead.

- *On her all-time favorite database...*My all-time favorite database is TP-ALL on Westlaw. I can't tell you how often I get a question, whether on a legal topic or something more basic like "What does this abbreviation mean?" and I plug in some search terms in TP-ALL, pull up a few articles and I'm done. TP-ALL is a huge database that includes law reviews, journals, Practising Law Institute program materials, and a number of treatises.

- *On keeping current with new Web resources...*Cornell has a service called InSITE that gathers new sites from a number of listservs and creates an annotated listing that is accessible several ways, including periodic notice by email. The ABA has something called Site-tation. At LLRX we do "Links in the News," which is about new resources.

- *On the imposition of a legal duty to search the Internet...*It's a little scary. Too seldom will the right resource be that obvious. It's truly not so easy to find some of what those cases consider "easily accessible." Even something you've stumbled upon before might not be that easy to find again. There is so much serendipity involved with the Internet.

- *On searching the Web differently than Westlaw or Lexis...*The people who have the hardest time with the search engines are those who approach them as if they were using Lexis or Westlaw. To some extent you have to be a lazy searcher and let the relevancy ranking do what it's supposed to do. You see people going into the search engines and doing these elaborate searches. That's probably one of the biggest mistakes.

Genie Tyburski

The Virtual Chase

Genie Tyburski is research librarian for the firm Ballard Spahr Andrews & Ingersoll, LLP. She manages *The Virtual Chase: A Research Site for Legal Professionals* and writes columns in *Law Office Computing* and *Law Library Resource Xchange* (LLRX). She speaks frequently at Internet, continuing legal education, and information industry programs. Ms. Tyburski received her master's degree in information studies from Drexel University. She is a member of the American Association of Law Libraries, Special Libraries Association, and the Pennsylvania Bar Association Technology Task Force. *Any statements, representations, inferences, or impressions are those of Genie Tyburski and do not reflect upon the practices, policies, or opinions of Ballard Spahr Andrews & Ingersoll, LLP.*

tyburski@virtualchase.com
www.virtualchase.com

How did you get into legal research?

I fell into it. I got a dual degree in history and Spanish, and felt educated but unemployable. I had worked in an academic library for three years while an undergraduate, and decided that was a skill one could market. Reference librarians seemed to have an interesting job. They were answering questions all day long, any question, out of the blue. I wanted to research and write, so I went to library school at Drexel. I also took a job with Community Legal Services, cataloging their collection. About six months into the job, the library director quit and recommended me for her position. I said, "You did what?" She gave me a crash course in two weeks on the importance of every single book in that library. I started answering questions almost immediately because they had five libraries and only one professional librarian. At the same time, Lexis [54, see Appendix A] was just coming into Legal Services. I had to learn how to use Lexis so I could teach others. They made me the permanent librarian and, after I got my library science degree, a position opened with a law firm.

How did your Web site, *The Virtual Chase*, get started?

I had been at Ballard Spahr about a year and a half, we were on the Internet, and my impression was, "This is the future." In 1994 I decided to teach myself hypertext markup language (HTML). I had been writing since the start of my career, so I decided I could put my articles on a Web site. That was the basis of *The Virtual Chase* [3]. In 1995 it was becoming more obvious that there were certain things on the Internet that law librarians probably ought to know about, like EDGAR [11]. I started to write about these things, mostly for local trade association journals. I wrote a lot about the Internet. All of a sudden, I was getting calls from all around the country. "I heard about your article on such and such. Can I have a copy? Can you fax it to me?" That was flattering at first, but soon it became a burden. So I replicated the publication versions of the articles as nearly as I could on the Web site.

In October of 1996, I decided to add more value to the Web site. I was doing a lot of writing about other Web sites that had good quality information for researchers. I created *The Annotated Guide to Resources for Legal Professionals*. In its original form it was one long page of annotated resources. Somewhere around the fall of 1996, I decided it needed a name other than Genie Tyburski's Web Site. What was I going to call this thing? I wanted to convey that it was a research site. My focus is strategies for finding information. I needed a name to convey that. In the shower one day, where some of the best thinking goes on, I said, "Paper Chase. This is an electronic version of *The Paper Chase*, that movie and TV show about law school. So it became *The Virtual Chase*. It now has more than 500 pages of information dealing with the strategy of finding information.

Tell us about the setting where you're working now.

I am the research librarian for Ballard Spahr. I'm the contact person for research consultation, or for actually doing the research, depending on the needs of the lawyer. We have about 190 attorneys locally and about 300 nationwide. Sometimes the librarians from the other offices, or their lawyers, contact me for consultation, but the majority of the work I do is local. It comes to me in all different forms: email, telephone, walk-in or memo. It can be as mundane as "I need a copy of a case" to something really complex like "I've got a client faced with this issue and I'm not sure where to go from here. What I've done hasn't helped. Do you have any suggestions?" Those tend to be non-legal research questions. A lot of the purely legal research is handled by the associates, but certain lawyers prefer to have legal research done by the librarians. Those lawyers usually either come into the office, or invite me or one of my colleagues into a meeting with their client, where they discuss the issues and ask me to research specific questions.

Do you have an intake procedure for that?

I wouldn't call it a procedure. We do a reference interview. There is no formula to it. It's a conversation. You come to me, you need information, and it's my job to figure out why you need it and how you're going to use it, so I can give you the *best* information. Typically, someone will come in and say "I need to know everything about ABC Company." "Okay, why?" You have to do it in such a way that it doesn't sound like an attack. If it's a securities attorney, I might start with something like, "Is your client doing a deal with this company? If I understand you correctly, you need to know its financial stability." I try to narrow and focus the request through the reference interview. The questions you ask depend on the issue. In recent years it has become more important to know "When do you need it?" and "In what form?" Earlier, I would pull down a couple of books, a couple of articles — a big stack of material — carry them up to your office and say

"Here." It wasn't an answer. It was information. Today they want an answer. Since it's an answer, how do you want that answer? Do you want the supporting documentation? Do you need it in electronic form, or in hardcopy, or do you just want a verbal answer?

Your turnaround times are quite rapid?

They have to be, because that's what's being requested of the attorney. There are unrealistic expectations out there. The client is placing demands on the attorney. The attorney is attempting to be responsive, and so makes the same demands on the library staff.

Has the Internet affected your procedure at the reference interview stage?

It's affected procedure on a number of different levels. One is that email plays a role, now, in communication. That has both positives and negatives. The positive is that it's very quick, and it doesn't require that I be in the library to help one of my attorneys. You could say that of the telephone to a certain extent, but it's more common, now, for me to receive email and be able to respond at home or when I'm on the road. The downside is the level of communication and people's writing skills. Some people can convey what they mean very well in writing, and some people can't. The reference interview becomes much more difficult if you've got someone who can't write, and who won't return phone calls but will return email. It affects the reference interview in terms of expectations, too.

There is a lot of hype and misunderstanding about information on the Internet. A lot of people believe you just sit down at the computer and say, "I need an answer to this question." Speak the question and the computer responds; that's the Internet. The expectations have risen very, very high for turnaround times. The idea that I'm sitting there waiting for work, and not currently involved in something else so I can be instantaneously responsive, is a fallible one. The idea that I can just tap a couple of keys and get that information spit right out is a problem the Internet is responsible for. The idea that all information is on the Internet is another problem we encounter quite often. We do background investigations on people our clients are dealing with. A typical question will be, "I need a criminal check done on so and so." What the attorney typically doesn't understand is that there is no national system for finding out whether someone's been a criminal on a federal, state or local level. The reference interview now becomes an education process. I have to say, "Where has your guy been?" "Well, I don't know. His name is Joe Smith. Do a background check." "What's Joe Smith's social security number?" "I don't know." "Date of birth?" "I don't know." So we have to find all that data first. Then we have to say, for example, "He's primarily in the Philadelphia area. We can do a criminal check here in Philadelphia County, but that's not going to pick up any convictions in the surrounding counties or in the state, because there's no statewide system in Pennsylvania for checking criminal records. That's not going to tell me whether he's ever been in any federal prison. If your guy's in Florida, we can do a statewide criminal check." It's confusing to the attorneys why sometimes we can respond instantaneously, and sometimes we can't.

Are there times when you start researching what was settled on at the reference interview stage and, as you're getting into it, think to yourself, "Wait a minute, I wonder if we're researching the right question? Should I stop here and talk again with the attorney?"

It happens a lot. An ideal scenario between a patron and a researcher is one with constant communication. Questions come up often. I can give you an example of one I had this week: We've got a judgment against a defendant. We want to collect on the judgment. Does this person have any money? The person's attorney says no. So what does the lawyer do? My recommendation is to do an asset check. The lawyer went onto Lexis, searched properties, and found a couple of properties that were recently transferred out of this person's name. What she doesn't know is whether there are any other assets, or whether the individual on the property record is the defendant. She comes to me asking how she can verify that Ms. X of the judgment is Ms. X who transferred these properties. We have an email reference interview in which I first have to elicit what she knows about the person they have the judgment against. I need the full name. I need the social security number and date of birth. I need the last known address. Any one of those will help me get started. She has the last known address, so that's enough to get started with the verification angle. But the question behind the one presented is, did her original asset search cover all possible assets? In my point of view, it didn't. She went onto Lexis and she searched properties. She didn't do any manual searching. She didn't search any other online systems. She didn't search anything beyond real property. My job is to educate her that there are other kinds of assets out there, that there are other ways to get at that information, that Lexis isn't the be-all and end-all.

Does this happen also in strictly legal research?

It happens most when the answer I'm finding is not the answer they want. I try to look for analogies. Maybe there's another angle we've overlooked. That usually requires that I have more knowledge of their litigation situation, or of the client situation. Usually the only information I have is the question they want answered. Whether I can help them depends on their attitude toward me as a librarian. Most attorneys think of librarians as professionals and professional researchers, but not all of them fully understand that giving me all the information they have helps me do a better job for them.

I wonder if associates, because of what they know about law, might be too quick to pigeonhole the issue.

That would filter what they're looking for in legal research.

I see it as a broader problem. I don't think it is necessarily because they're lawyers. I think it is, in part, a generational issue. The younger generation has grown up with shortcuts and technology. I've given a lot of thought to this. I see it in my own kids. Just recently, a new lawyer said to me, "I am much more productive if I take a question to the computer. I can key in my search terms so that I get an answer. But if I go and I stand in the library, look at the digests and treatises, I'm very unproductive. I'm flipping around. I don't know how to use these tools, and I'm not getting an answer. Why I should do any manual research?" You're not going to hear that from very many lawyers over the age of thirty. My response was, "I believe your skills are good enough to go on the computer and get an answer, but what are you missing along the way?" There is so much out there, and they have learned to weed through it. They're not bothered by getting 300 email messages a day, because they can zap out and get down to the one percent that's of value to them, faster than you or I can change our clothes. It's the way they think. But, because of the way they think, they miss the big picture. They can zero in better than you or I, but they don't see relationships and they don't take time to think about things. They have their answer but they might not have the complete answer, or the best answer to help the case.

On the other hand, we have the older lawyer who is uncomfortable with computers, is comfortable with books, and who can see the big picture and see relationships. He can get an answer also, but he will miss things, too. He will miss them because there's a lot of information in electronic form that previously was not easily obtainable without great expense. They used to pass it up because, if you couldn't obtain it easily, the other guy couldn't obtain it easily either, so it wasn't something to worry about.

What triggers the decision to use electronic research?

I wish I had an answer for that, but I don't think it's black and white. Most research of a truly legal question requires a combination of approaches. Extenuating circumstances might make the decision for you. Time is a big factor. We have less of it as a case goes on. Money is another factor. Will the client pay for it? I often argue that it will cost more to walk across town and get that book from a library, yet the client doesn't want to pay for me to pull it off the computer. If we don't have a lot of time, I'm likely to jump online because it's faster. I'd give all kinds of disclaimers with that information. I have had to put aside some of my principles, I guess. I like to be thorough. I like to be correct. But you've got a client on the phone waiting for the answer, or you've got them in a conference room with the attorney waiting for an answer, so you can't always be as thorough as you would like.

Are you asked to estimate the cost of projects?

All the time. I find that very difficult. Often there is a direct correlation between cost and the amount of information you find. You can't know that in advance. I usually say, "Give me a starting budget" or "Your starting budget has to be X amount," depending on the question. I charge for my time, and there are charges for the resources and other expenses, so you're probably looking at $300 as a usual minimum for any kind of project. I say, "Let me see what I can find within that budget, and then I'll tell you what is left to be done." It's a negotiation process. Sometimes, we can get a sufficient answer within that minimal budget. Other times, when they see what we've found in that first phase, they release additional budget.

Law schools teach stock approaches to formulating research strategies. What is your impression of those?

It is like putting a square peg in a round hole, because it assumes that research is a science, and it's not. It's an art. What you do, and the order in which you do it, depend on the information being asked for. Some things *are* close to being a formula, like updating case law. But most research is thinking, being creative about the way you might get that information, being persistent. Rarely can I say, "If you have this question, you need to do this." That's not to say there's nothing I've done over and over, but when you're looking for an answer to a question, I don't think there's a formula. There are some basic skills that can be taught. You can be taught how to use a digest, or how to formulate a keyword search, but you cannot be taught how to think. You cannot be taught how to analyze, how to draw relationships. That's aptitude. If you don't have that, you're missing a key factor in being a good researcher.

Say you're trying to find the current state of Pennsylvania law on a certain point. Can you make a general statement on the approach you use?

First, find out if there's any statutory law on the point. This is where law school makes a mistake in how it teaches research. A new lawyer comes in, he's got a legal question, and right away he's thinking case law. My response is, "Is there an answer in the statutes?" Then, find out if there's an accompanying regulation or some interpretation of that statute. Take, for example, an indictment for mail fraud by overbilling. What is overbilling? Is what he did really mail fraud? Now you have an issue to research under that statute, and then you look at your annotations to get your case law: Here's a case that says something on the issue of overcharging. Then you try to find other similar cases, or you use Shepherd's or KeyCite. Depending on the specific question, there could be a best approach — not necessarily the only approach, but a best approach. Often, it begins with statutes and branches out from there, depending on what you find. You come into the cases through the annotations.

Suppose you find there is no applicable statute. What is your approach?

It still might be something of a regulatory nature. If not, before going to case law, I go to treatises and articles. I try to find some commentary to get me started. The commentary usually cites the leading cases. If it's an area of law that I've researched a lot, and I feel comfortable with the digests and keywords, I might go directly to the West digest. If I am not clear about the substance of the legal issues, I might start with an American Law Reports (ALR) annotation. If I don't find an ALR annotation, my next step, typically, is the encyclopedia. I go to ALR first because they tend to be more practical. The encyclopedias tend to be more academic.

Are you sometimes asked to "get everything on" a certain topic?

All the time. We're so pressed for time that we don't think about what we really want. It's easier to send an email message, because then you're not going to be confronted by this librarian who has questions. They always have questions. Those questions are sometimes a source of frustration for our patrons. They don't understand the reason for those questions. So we'll get an email message, "Get me everything on…." My typical reply is, "Are you looking for A, B, or C?" I don't ask, "What specifically are you looking for?" because the response would be "Everything."

Let's say they are looking for information on an individual. "Are you interested in knowing this person's expertise, occupational background, whether they've been quoted in the news, whether there's dirt about them?" I try to be very specific and lean on them to get an answer. Hopefully, it will cause them to think about the question a little more. "What I really need to know, because this guy is a member of a class, is whether he is a professional litigant." Something like that really changes the nature of the question. I never accept questions at face value. That kind of question definitely needs a reference interview.

If you're doing research on Lexis or Westlaw [60], how much planning do you do before you log on?

I become as familiar as I can with the substance of the question before I go online. That means doing some research in the books. That gives me a greater understanding of the question, and some keywords. The way the lawyer who made the research request describes it may be different from the way the judges describe it in their opinions. When they say, "This is the term of art," that may be true, but this term of art isn't always used, and sometimes it's "canine" instead of "dog."

How do you build a search?

It depends on your knowledge of the topic and your perception of the information that might be available. If I think I know what it's about, and I think there ought to be information out there, I start narrow. I try to zero right in on it. If I don't have a good handle on the subject, I start very broad, because I'm going to try to educate myself along the way. It may become apparent that I need to get offline and consult some basic treatises. Sometimes, certain key phrases will jump out and tell me, "This is what I want to look for. This is how to narrow my request."

If I'm on Lexis, I might use the Focus feature. It's much more useful than the Modification feature that wipes out your original search. Sometimes I want to go back and look at earlier results. I like the Westlaw Locate feature for the same reason. Using both of those features assumes that I don't have to re-write the search entirely, which I may have to do if I started with an erroneous understanding of the subject or an erroneous assumption of some kind.

Which record format do you look at first?

On Lexis, KWIC (Key Word In Context) is a favorite format. I also like to look at bibliographic information, because dates are important, sometimes more important than author or title. With news articles, twenty-five words of context are usually sufficient. With other kinds of information, and depending on how much I know about the subject, I may have to expand the context to make sure I'm getting exactly what I want.

When do you limit your searches to certain segments or fields?

I frequently search news articles by headline and lead paragraph. For author searches, I search the author field. I use subject terms a lot outside of Lexis and Westlaw. If I'm on Dialog [48] or Medline via Grateful Med [13], I like to look at the thesaurus. The thesaurus works well in congressional information, also. Let's say you want to do as much of a legislative history as you can electronically. On the federal level, Thomas [15] is not the authoritative source of that information, but it is better developed than the GPO site [12] with respect to search features and additional information like commentary and status. Thomas has a thesaurus called Legislative Indexing Vocabulary. Suppose I need to find pending legislation on the death penalty. I can go into the Legislative Indexing Vocabulary and find how the legislative analysts index that topic. They index it under "capital punishment." Instead of searching on "death penalty," it will be more productive to search on "capital punishment."

How often do you use the documentation for online services?

I feel comfortable formulating searches on Lexis, Westlaw and Dialog without looking at the documentation. When I'm working outside of those systems, I have the documentation right next to me and consult it regularly. Some systems like Dow Jones [49] use both a WITHIN connector and a NEAR connector. What is the difference, and will I remember it the next time I use the service? I might think I remember, but that can be dangerous, so I always have that documentation handy. Sometimes the name of a function on one service has a different meaning on another service. NEAR on Dow Jones means WITHIN on Lexis. WITHIN on Dow Jones means PRECEDE on Lexis. It can get confusing. They supply a one-page summary of their Boolean connectors and so forth. I keep that handy.

How about quality of information on the Internet?

Quality problems arise frequently on the Web. Sometimes I think it is intentional. Technology facilitates trickery. I have seen Web sites with reproductions of commercial information, perhaps an article, with no copyright permission granted. I question whether I can rely on that source, because it's not authentic. It's not the publisher offering the article; it's Joe Blow at America Online offering a copy of the article. What if he's got a Web site on a particular issue that relates to the article, and his point of view is very strong in one direction? What if he's changed that article? I have found a case where that was done. It changed the whole slant of the article. The article was an interview, and the thoughts were changed in such a way as to put emphasis on things that were not emphasized in the original article. The Web version had graphics and photographs that were not in the original article. It had an ending that was not in the original article, an interview with somebody giving an opposing point of view. But it was presented on the Web as though it were a copy of the article.

You do Internet training. Do you look for examples of this to warn your students?

Yes. Whether I'm giving an hour or six hours, you're going to get a lecture on the quality of information. So I look for these things. Tass.net is a Web site [www.tass.net/] presented as a newswire. The "Top Story" is noted as having been "Filed by TASS Newswire staff: Tuesday July 1, 1997," so it's not very current, already. The headline is "Pol Pot Reconfirms Presence in Stockholm, Sweden." It opens with a paragraph purportedly quoting Pol Pot saying, "I should know where I am better than anyone else." The story says he had eluded his captors and, with the help of an organization called Komintern, has made it into Sweden. At the top are links for Top Story, Newswire, Archives and Corporate Info. At the bottom are links to Background Story and a video. At the top is a banner for Tass.net, which you can click to go to the homepage. If you click for the homepage, you get that exact same page. When you click on the Corporate Information link, you get a page telling you this is TASS InfoWerk, a newswire service you can subscribe to for the latest and greatest in news. If you click on the link for the background story [www.tass.net/index 2.html] you get a page with one link for Komintern. Click on that and you get a very Soviet Union kind of graphic page [http://www.komintern.se/], but then it becomes obvious that this is a Web hosting and design service that believes getting someone's attention on the Web requires radical methods.

So the news story is a hoax, but you don't know that unless you know about the topic to begin with, or unless you click on the link for the background and then click on Komintern. You have to look at this site with more care than you would in the physical world because, in a library, the assumption is that an evaluation process has taken place already.

You have to read the site's purpose statement, if it offers one. You have to know why they're out there. My grandmother puts up a Web site — why is she is doing it? If you don't know why, you have no basis for judging the information. That's number one. Number two is the date of the information. If you can't determine that, I don't think it's useable information. You have to consider completeness, objectivity and point of view — all that is important. For newspapers, there are often many differences between the print version and the Web version. Sometimes you may feel comfortable with a print resource. You may think, for example, that you know *Martindale-Hubbell* [56] inside and outside. If you want to get a lawyer's bio, you know right where to go. But that product on the Web is not an exact replicate of the product in print. You can't make the assumption that it is without reading the site documentation. If you read the site documentation, which is very good at *Martindale-Hubbell,* it will tell you there are no Iowa listings here, there are no attorney ratings here, there are no state law digests here, and on and on. The site needs to document that for researchers. If that documentation isn't there, I don't think it's safe to assume that product is the same on the Web as it is in print.

What about data quality problems stemming from the process of converting a document from one electronic format to another?

This actually came up in a meeting with some new lawyers today. We were talking about EDGAR. When an attorney in this firm creates a document to be filed with the SEC, they create it in WordPerfect. Then they send it out to a printer who EDGARizes it and sends it back. The attorneys have to proof the document again. They were complaining about that. They didn't understand why, when they get it back, some words or some numbers are in the wrong place. That happens because you're converting one electronic product into another electronic product. It's another example of how important it is to proof and verify when you're working with electronic documents. When you're working with numbers that are going to be filed with the SEC for a public company, and you've got a line item that says 1,000 but it's supposed to say 1,000,000, that's a problem.

How much do you use the Internet?

I use the Internet more than anything else. I have to define "Internet" because it connotes the "World Wide Web" and "free." Both of those are erroneous. First, the Internet is much more than the Web, and secondly, a lot of the good quality information out there is not free. I use commercial and subscription services via the

Web. I don't have to learn new proprietary software. I get comfortable with Netscape, Internet Explorer, Opera, or whatever the latest craze is, and that's all I have to get comfortable with. That's one reason I tend to gravitate toward the Web. For example, I used to access Dow Jones by dialing up through Tymnet. I used ProComm Plus. Now I navigate to Dow Jones Interactive on the Web because I prefer the interface. Dun & Bradstreet [50] is another example. We used to access it through a dial-up number with ProComm Plus. Now it's on the Web. This is the future. I think it behooves us to get comfortable with the Web product if one is available. I include Westlaw and Lexis in that. Speed is an issue, though. Unstable technology, like Java scripts, is another problem.

Where else do you go on the Internet to do legal research?

It depends on the nature of the question. For one of our clients we wanted to get an easily understandable article on a certain type of investment tool, the real estate investment trust, or REIT. The lawyer's explanation was not understandable to the client. I went onto Lexis-Nexis, did a search — nothing, zero. I thought, "My gosh, *Business Lawyer* has to have something on this." It didn't. I even checked the manual index, just in case my searching was off. Nothing. Westlaw — nothing. Dialog — nothing. Dow Jones — nothing. In desperation I said, "I gotta get in touch with a trade association. There has to be something on this." I went onto Yahoo! [66] to see if I could find a trade association that would be relevant to this particular investment tool, and sure enough, I did. Yahoo! had a link to a very good Web site, NAREIT (National Association of Real Estate Investment Trusts) Online [97]. They have an archive of articles. I found two on REITs, written so I could understand them. The attorney was overjoyed. The moral of the story is not to underrate the value of trade associations and their Web sites.

We used to subscribe to a commercial service that sold just congressional documents. We stopped subscribing after GPO Access and Thomas had been available on the Web for about a year. That's not to say there's no value in the commercial service, but we used it for document retrieval, for finding similar legislation, and for getting status information. You can do all that with Thomas and GPO Access.

Are there times when failure to use Internet research would be incompetent?

Oh, yeah. Absolutely. I would have been incompetent had I not given the attorney those investment tool articles I found on the Web. Without that, I would have gone back to him empty-handed. That kind of trade association publication often is held close to the chest in the print world. They aren't online anywhere but the Web.

Let's say you've got a client who wants to renovate an historic building, and in the process of renovation he wants to put in both apartments and small business offices. Does he have to comply with the Americans with Disabilities Act? You look at the statute and believe it could be interpreted a number of different ways. You look at the regulations, such as they are. You look at a treatise and find it overly broad and not dealing with your issue. The answer is not in the statutes, the regulations or the treatises. Where do you go? If you go to the Department of Justice, Civil Division [17], you're going to find their Freedom of Information Act library [18]. All the FOIA letters to the DOJ with respect to the ADA are there, and you find one that has the same fact scenario as your client's. There is no search facility; you have to click through them, but what if this were in the print world? You might write the Department of Justice and say, "Under the Freedom of Information Act, I would like all of your letters on this issue." You're going to have to go through them one by one anyway. So what's the difference? If you don't think about the resources available on the Web, yes, in most cases you would be incompetent.

How about incompetence and the currency of information on the Web?

I wrote an article about that in response to a reader's question, "How can I do federal statutory and regulatory research on the Web and know I'm getting current information?" I chose an example where the regulation had been amended. The amendment had not yet made it into the print edition, but was on GPO Access. The *Federal Register* is available there on the day of publication at 6 a.m. You can't get any more current than that. It takes at least two days for the *Federal Register* to arrive in print. You can't get New Jersey's statutes in any more current form than you can on the New Jersey legislative Web site [21], which is updated daily. They don't incorporate every chapter law on a daily basis, but they are more current on the Web site than on Lexis, Westlaw, Premise [104], or any other product I've checked.

Have you ever been able to satisfy a search request using only the Internet?

That usually happens when I'm looking for an interpretive document written by a federal agency. State agencies in some states are very good about posting this information as well. Suppose I need an Environmental Protection Agency [19] guidance memo. I can get that on the Web, and nowhere else electronically. In fact, I can't even get it from the EPA because they won't give it to me anymore. They refer me to the Web site.

We needed a definition of the various levels of security within prisons. The lawyer called the Bureau of Prisons [16] and was told that the information is on the Web. But the Web site is not easy to navigate. She was unable to find the document and called them back asking, "Can't you just fax it to me?" The response was, "No, it's on the Web site. If you want us to send you a print copy, you have to send a written Freedom of Information Act request." So she came to me and she had the document in ten minutes. These documents are not easily obtainable in the print world.

Another example is briefs and law firm memos. Some law firms offer some of their research memos on their Web sites, or via other Web sites like *Law Journal EXTRA* [88]. I can find my lawyers a model document on an issue. I'm not going to find that on Lexis or Westlaw. Suppose we're going up against Company A, the issue is X and, right there on Company A's Web site, they affirm whatever they are denying in the lawsuit. It's evidence, and we've used that.

Are there reasons to use Lexis or Westlaw on the Web and not via their proprietary software?

For Westlaw I prefer the proprietary software because of the slowness of the Internet, particularly in the afternoon. Westlaw's proprietary software is superior to their competitors', in my opinion. Lexis has done a much better job with their Web product than they did with their proprietary software. Two features on Lexis are available only via their Web product, and only with a version 4.x or higher browser. They're called More Like This and More Like Selected Text. Let's say statutory law covers an issue. I look at the case annotations, find a case that closely relates to my issue, and pull it up with a Get A Document command. With a click of the More Like This button, I get a screen that allows me to define what More Like This means. Do I want more cases that cite the same or similar cases, or do I want more cases with a language pattern similar to this case? Do I want to further define it by entering mandatory terms, terms that have to appear in the case? More Like This gives me an additional handful, up to fifty cases, that are similar in concept to the case that was previously on the monitor. I look through those cases, find one that says exactly what I want it to say, highlight the sentences, and then click on More Like Selected Text. I love that. That is futuristic. I've been very impressed with the relevancy of the cases that come up using those features. I always have to consider content, though, because the content is not the same as you get through the proprietary software at this time.

Are there Internet sites you often start with, regardless of the legal issue being researched?

No, because I have to think about what you're asking for and the most direct route from point A to point B. That's the route I'm going to take. I have a lot of known sources. If, in a particular instance, I don't have a known source, there are certain starting places I might try, such as FindLaw [6] or CataLaw [5]. I stay away from search engines. Although they probably contain a lot of quality data, it's very difficult to extract it. It's often interwoven with pages and pages of irrelevant data and broken links. Their ranking algorithms leave a bit to be desired, and that's not even taking spamming into account.

Even the catalogs or directories have serious drawbacks. I have a lot of respect for FindLaw. I appreciate their commitment to the legal profession. They offer a lot of excellent products for free, like Legal News and Legal Minds. But take a look at their catalog of legal Web sites; it's a junkyard. They include any and every Web site that has anything remotely to do with law. In my assessment, there is no evaluation taking place. Let's take a look at this resource that says it's discussing lemon laws. What is the expertise or authority behind this site? Lawyers who are not taught to think that way go to FindLaw as if it were the be-all and end-all of legal information on the Web. I have a problem with it. CataLaw has a more discriminatory selection, but a lot of good Web sites are not included. It is a problem for Webmasters to index the quality information out there. They can't keep up with it.

Do you use any of the client software that is promoted as being adapted particularly to legal research?

I tried one of them. It was pretty decent for novices. It was very Alexa-like [103]. While you were at a Web site, it would pop up automatically and tell you what sites you had visited in the past that contained related information. I think all these products tend to suffer from the same problems as search engines. They're dependent on the data they are able to collect. Netscape 4.5 has a feature called What's

Related that uses Alexa technology. If I'm at *Law Library Resource Xchange* (LLRX) [1] and click on What's Related, I get a list of ten law-related Web sites, such as *The Internet Lawyer* [83], that offer news commentary. If I'm at *The Virtual Chase*, it tells me there's nothing out there that's related. I can interpret that as, "Wow! I have a wonderful, unique site that no one has been able to duplicate," or I can face the real world and say that Alexa doesn't know about *The Virtual Chase*. It's the same problem with search engines: What's indexed and what isn't, and how relevant is it? What algorithm are they using to determine relevance? I've gotten some pretty oddball What's Related results when I click on that feature.

Have you ever looked for something you felt sure had to be on the Web but you never were able to find it?

I can't tell you how many times I have come across information on the Internet and said, "Oh, I am so glad to know that's there. I know I'm going to need that sometime." It may be the next day — and I can't find it. Through Dogpile [62], I had found case law where this individual was an expert. I had found that this individual's wife had a homepage. Through that wife's homepage I found that this individual was a member of XY & Z organization. I found that certain transcript services had information on this individual. I got interrupted and I didn't download the data. I went back the next day and Dogpile had nothing on this individual. Nothing. Why does that happen? Sometimes it can happen if it is a busy time of day and Dogpile is truncating the retrieval from all the search engines it covers. But it didn't matter what time of day I did this search; I could not reproduce it. I had to manually find all those sites, and one of them I never could find again.

How do you handle data output from the Internet?

It depends on where I am when I do the research, and what the attorney said he wanted. If I'm working in the office, I usually print it, hand the attorney a copy, and it's up to him to keep it. I don't save it electronically. I can't keep everything I do research on. I realized that a couple of years ago. There is not enough file space, and I never *have* referred back to anything. By the time they'd come back with a question or get back to me and say, "I lost it," the search would have to be done again because of the speed with which information changes.

If I'm out of the office, I am more likely to save a search to disk and upload it to email. I have to use File Save As in my browser for every page, and I have to remember to do that for the graphics as well. Then I have to change the HTML because it's not pointing to the graphics where I saved them. I used to use WebWhacker. I would do an outline in HTML, whack those pages, create the links to them, and send it off by email. Then WebWhacker changed its software and I didn't like it, so I stopped using it. Now I use Front Page, import what I need, and sometimes I can even get Front Page to recalculate the links to the graphics for me. You move the files and it says, "Do you want to rename the links?" Sometimes that works. Sometimes I use a Replace All command. It's more work than we had to do in the past to present information, but it's not a lot of work.

Do you bookmark a lot of sites for fear that you won't be able to find them again?

How many times do you use the same resource in a library? That's the way I feel about Web sites. There are certain ones that I'm going to use frequently, like CataLaw and FindLaw as starting points, or LLRX to get up to date on the latest technology issues. If I run across a tremendous database at the Federal Reserve that tells me everything I ever wanted to know about the balance sheets of banks of all kinds, it's a tremendous resource but I'm not going to bookmark it. How many times am I going to need it? If I don't remember it's the Federal Reserve, I know it's a federal agency.

What is that agency likely to be? There's a limited number that I have to check.

I try to avoid information overload, and bookmarks can become exactly that. They become outdated very quickly because of the way links change. I have my commercial sites bookmarked, and they very rarely change. The rest of the bookmarking I do is related to my writing. I have folders for the publications I write for, and I drop things in that I use while working on a writing project.

How is the Internet affecting the role of the legal research specialist or the law librarian?

I am seeing a wave of individuals who have tried to do it themselves and have found that it's not everything it's cracked up to be. I hear a lot of frustration from attorneys: "The Internet is not what I expected. I had to weed through thirty pages of links at HotBot [64] and I found information of minimal value." When they get to that point, if they've left us in the library, they're coming back. Some are way too much into the hype, and are not giving much consideration to the consultation we offer. These are individuals I'm talking about, not large numbers of lawyers, and I fear for them, because they have blinders on.

How do you decide where to stop a search if you're still finding things?

I stop if I get an answer. In today's world, that's all they want. Ten years ago, a mound of paper was sufficient to answer a question. Today all they want is one page. Usually, I offer to do more. I'll say, "This is an answer. I'm sure that additional information exists, and I'd be happy to continue the research." I'm very rarely taken up on that. Sometimes money will stop me; that's very frustrating because I will have gotten so close, the budget is spent, and the client won't budge. The client is satisfied but I *know* there's something else out there. Maybe that "something else" is a problem for the client. Time is another factor. Sometimes what they want just can't be done in the time they have.

What can a patron do, in bringing you a research request, to help you do the best job for them?

Communication. Tell me everything they know. Don't hold anything back. Talk to me. Answer my questions. Be patient. Demands on their time and demands from clients can hold them back. If the client comes with an unrealistic demand, the attorney comes with an unrealistic demand. This is a very impatient society. This is a society suffering from information overload and a feeling of incompetence because of the technology required today to do one's job. There is a lot of stress in the workplace and communication isn't what it should be.

Super Searcher Secrets

- *On Internet hype...*A lot of people believe you just sit down at the computer and say, "I need an answer to this question." Speak the question and the computer responds. That's the Internet. The expectations have risen very, very high for turnaround times. The idea that I can just tap a couple of keys and get that information spit right out is a problem the Internet is responsible for. The idea that all information is on the Internet is another problem we encounter quite often.

- *On stock research approaches...*Stock research approaches taught in law schools are like putting a square peg in a round hole because it assumes that research is a science, and it's not. It's an art. What you do, and the order in which you do it, depend on the information being asked for. Most research is thinking, being creative about the way you might get that information, being persistent.

- *On the typical starting point...*First, find out if there's any statutory law on the point. This is where law school makes a mistake in how it teaches research. A new lawyer comes in, he's got a legal question, and right away he's thinking case law. My response is, "Is there an answer in the statutes?" Then find out if there's an accompanying regulation or some interpretation of that statute.

- *On consulting documentation...*When I'm working outside Lexis, Westlaw, and Dialog, I have the documentation right next to me and consult it regularly. Some systems like Dow Jones use both a WITHIN connector and a NEAR connector. What is the difference? Can I remember that the next time I use the service? Sometimes the name of a function on one service has a different meaning on another service. NEAR on Dow Jones means WITHIN on Lexis. WITHIN on Dow Jones means PRECEDE on Lexis.

- *On information quality on the Internet...*Quality problems happen more frequently on the Web than is noted. Sometimes I think it is intentional. Technology facilitates trickery. I have seen Web sites with reproductions of commercial information. It's Joe Blow at America Online offering me a copy of the article. What if he's changed that article? It can be done. I have found a case where that was done. It changed the whole slant of the article.

- *On bookmarking Web sites...*How many times do you use the same resource in a library? That's the way I feel about Web sites. If I run across a tremendous database at the Federal Reserve that tells me everything I ever wanted to know about the balance sheets of banks of all kinds, it's a tremendous resource, but I'm not going to bookmark it. If I don't remember it's the Federal Reserve, I know it's a federal agency. What is that agency likely to be? There's a limited number that I have to check.

- *On how the Internet affects the role of the research specialist...*I am seeing a wave of individuals who have tried to do it themselves and have found that it's not everything it's cracked up to be. I hear a lot of frustration from attorneys. "I had to weed through thirty pages of links at HotBot and I found information of minimal value." When they get to that point, if they've left us, they're coming back.

Photograph by Glogau Studio, Bethesda, MD. Used by permission.

Roberta I. Shaffer

Library as Hub of the Firm

Roberta I. Shaffer is dean of the Graduate School of Library and Information Science at the University of Texas at Austin. At the time of this interview, she was director of Research Information Services at the Washington office of Covington & Burling. She has worked at the Library of Congress, George Washington University Law School, and the University of Houston Law Center. For the past several years, she has been an adjunct professor at the Catholic University School of Library and Information Science. She is vice-president of the International Association of Law Libraries, and an active member of the American Association of Law Libraries. She is the editor of *Introduction to Transnational Legal Transactions* (Oceana, 1995), and serves on Oceana's Technology Board of Advisors. She is a graduate of Vassar College, has a library degree from Emory University, and a law degree from Tulane. *Any statements, representations, inferences, or impressions are those of Roberta I. Shaffer and do not reflect upon the practices, policies, or opinions of Covington & Burling.*

rshaffer@gslis.utexas.edu

How did you get into legal research?

I was enrolled in law school, anticipating a career in legal journalism, when I had a serious accident with a horse. I was unable to do anything but lie totally flat on my back or stand up. I couldn't sit. I had to leave law school. While I was in a pain clinic in Atlanta, Georgia, my father was concerned about my recovery. One day he went to Emory University's main library and saw a bunch of people walking around the reference area with sheets of paper. He stopped a young woman and asked, "What are you doing with these sheets of paper?" They were library school students. He asked, "Do you have to sit down?" This young woman said, "Oh no, if you major in reference, all you need to do is walk around a reference collection. Through the semester, the questions get increasingly more difficult. You use more books to answer the questions, but you probably would never have to sit down." My father came running back to my hospital room and said "I have found the perfect way for you to rehabilitate."

So, while I was taking physical therapy, I was also taking library school classes. At the end of library school, though I still loved to write, even more super-duper and more exciting was doing research. I decided that I would go back to law school, thinking there must be a way to marry the two careers. But that didn't seem quite as exciting to me after law school as did plain vanilla law librarianship.

Where did you learn more about research, library school or law school?

Library school. Law school focuses on teaching people to think like lawyers. That's an analytical way of thinking, approaching problem-solving in a certain manner, and being able to read in a certain critical way. I feel very fortunate having a background in both. I have the analytical underpinning from law school and the skill in approaching material critically from library school. In law school you didn't analyze materials by analyzing their sources.

In your job now, what is the place of the library in the firm?

The man who hired me had a vision of information, of the pivotal role that the library and the librarian would serve. Everybody here looked upon the library as the fulcrum of the firm. When they moved into this space in 1980, a lot of law firms were putting their libraries in basements or tucking them away in corners. They were not putting libraries in the heart of the firm. They never thought of putting our library anywhere but on the main floor, to serve as the hub of the firm. That way, as people would do research, they would talk with colleagues about what they were finding. This would be the "university" of the firm; all the ideas would come, in one way or another, from the library.

An important step was finding a way to integrate technology. By the 1990s, so many of our lawyers were not in the office a good part of their working day. They were out on the road litigating. Many of them were not even in the United States. There had to be a way for them to carry the university with them. This man, Stuart Stock, wanted me to come and help the firm get to that point.

How many librarians do you have here?

We have a staff of twenty-three, and half of us are librarians. Within that half, half are librarians with law degrees. The others either have extensive experience or an advanced degree in another discipline. While law itself is a discipline, the practice of law draws on any discipline imaginable. To do effective legal research, one must be crackerjack at doing research in any number of other disciplines.

How do research requests usually come in to the library?

They come in any way that man can communicate with man, predominantly by telephone or email. The lawyers are not in the office that much, and we have branch offices. Our preference is email. It's better to get spellings the way somebody believes something is spelled. It's better to memorialize the request in electronic form and build the file with that request as your beginning entry. We do get a lot of requests in person, in traditional reference interviews.

Since most of the requests come by email, how do you achieve the purposes of the reference interview?

If you are involved in the early phases of a lawyer's orientation at the firm, you can explain the kinds of things that are important to know in a research request, and the kinds of omissions that will totally skew the response. The reference interview itself then becomes less important. There's always going to be some ambiguity. Many times it's something you wouldn't realize yourself, even with a reference interview, until you've gotten started in the research. Many times there's an unbeknownst pitfall. The requestor doesn't know it, and *we* don't know it until we do some initial research. We don't want the client to be charged for our tracing rabbit trails. We can find the ambiguity by doing a little bit of research first. Then we're knowledgeable and can say, "Do you know that there are actually two strings one might pursue," or "We have discovered that there are two strings. Which one did you mean?"

This second contact is richer. Often the Internet is useful at this stage. We can get a sense of the controversies involved, if there are any, or the terminology, by popping onto the Net very quickly with no charge to the client except for the time it might take us. We might never go back to the Internet for that problem again, but it was a very useful first pass.

How quickly do you usually turn a project around?

In about sixty percent of our cases, they're asking for things they need today, or tomorrow at the latest. In the other forty percent, they are asking for research, as opposed to reference. A lot of places draw the distinction between reference and research based on the number of sources you use to answer the question. We do it on a time basis. We call something a reference question if we can find the answer completely within a day, and usually within an hour. We call something a research project if it would take us more than a twenty-four hour cycle to deliver the complete package.

Does the type of product you deliver depend on whether it's a reference request or a research project?

When it is a reference request, the product is an answer and the source. Most of the time we deliver it either on paper or electronically. We try not to give an oral answer and let it vanish with the user. Many times the user will not remember it by the time they need to use it, or may need to pass that information on to someone else. We don't want the game of "telephone" to distort the information.

When it's a research project, often we deliver not only the broad data, the raw research materials, but also an analysis of the veracity of the sources. That's why, many times, we have the lawyer librarians working on a project. We usually find the cases electronically and email them to the requestor right from Lexis [54, see Appendix A], Westlaw [60], or the Net, following our memo of analysis about the veracity of the materials they're getting. Not all judges in all circuits, not all law reviews and all treatises are created equal. Unfortunately, the political aspect of human nature often creeps into the beautiful, perfect legal system. We may want to explain why we have arranged the package with the number one document first, and the number ten document last.

Do you use checklists or pathfinders?

No. When people come to work for us, we try to have them in a "shadow" situation for several months. They watch the other librarians, learning how things are done here, and learning about the pitfalls in research. A great deal of our research is in non-U.S. law, where it is not clear what the sources are.

In our own country, there can be a similar effect if you're used to being a common law librarian and you're going to a state that is more code than not. California and New York are in many ways civil law jurisdictions. So much has been codified that it's not always intuitive how to do research in the New York code or the California code, even if you're a crackerjack researcher in other, standard codes. When somebody goes to the California code with the new librarian shadowing them, they realize that, gee, the procedure is a little bit different here. There may be a wholly separate code for certain subjects, not part of the big code. In certain jurisdictions, these things exist separately. In more code-intensive states, there may be a code that is just civil procedure, but you may need to look elsewhere for tangential issues, under another title. You need to be aware that if you just went to the big code and found things related to civil procedure, you're not even halfway home. There's another code, a commercial code or corporate code or something else, that has civil procedure aspects to it.

We have incorporated into our orientation — what we call an introductory period — this shadowing concept. You don't do anything without someone else overseeing your work for a period of time.

Let's say a librarian here is researching a question of law in an area where he or she has little background. Where should they start?

If you don't even know the key terms, you would start in the treatises, usually in paper. That's assuming that you really know nothing at all. That's what we advise our own requestors if they are coming to something as a new topic. That's so they can start sensing the issues and terminology, and identify some of the key cases. Increasingly, treatises are available on CD-ROM, on the Internet, and online. This is a fairly new phenomenon that has occurred in maybe the last six years for CD-ROM and the last three years, to any substantial extent, on Lexis, Westlaw, and the Internet. We're very big believers in KeyCiting and Shepardizing as a research entree.

You're not using citators just to validate the cases. You're using them to find the law.

Exactly. In fact, we often tell the lawyers that the *raison d'être* of KeyCite and Shepard's is as a research tool as well as a source validation tool. We would be hard-pressed to tell them which function is more important.

For a researcher with knowledge of a subject who still is somewhat uncertain, what would be the path?

We still would use secondary sources. We might take them to another level of treatise or loose-leaf service, or to a law review article. Often there are treatises or loose-leaf services that are more refined, not just *Williston on Contracts,* but somebody on common carrier contracts, or not just litigation, but class action litigation. The function here is as an entry point to the key cases and the key statutory or regulatory primary authority. We try to get people into the primary authority as quickly as we can, but in an organized fashion. That way is through treatises, loose-leaf services, or law reviews.

Law schools present stock strategies or approaches to performing legal research. What's your impression of those stock strategies?

There is not one recipe. Two big things — and several other lesser things — are always going to determine the ingredients of research. The first is the entry point of the research. You will take a different path, depending on where you fall along the scale from a novice to an expert researcher. The other critical item stems from the fact that some areas of law have developed on legal principles and other areas are driven by facts. If the question is a fact-based one, nine times out of ten I tell a researcher, at any level of expertise, to go online and do a keyword search with the facts as well-articulated as possible. If it's an area of law building on legal principles, we often keep them in the treatises and the law review articles, which tend not to be fact-based so much as legal principle based.

They don't tell you that in law school.

We know that because our brand-new associates always have a light bulb go on when we explain that to them. It's like, oh!

What factors trigger the use of electronic legal research instead of the paper library?

Where the researcher is, geographically, at the time. That would be a threshold question: Where are you and what kind of research sources do you have access to there? Next, is this an area of fact or of law? If it's an area of fact, we are more likely to go into electronic research almost right away. The treatises, the law reviews, and so on are not oriented toward that kind of research. They're not splitting hairs on facts so much as on law. It's not practical to send somebody to a treatise or a law review if it's really a fact-based situation.

Next is the comfort level of the researcher. Some people will never master loose-leaf services in paper. Something as basic as the fact that it's got paragraph and page numbers on the same page will always trap those researchers. They are going to lose direction and lose interest quickly in paper, because they're always going to be trapped by that simple thing, that we would never send them there. That is a CCH (Commerce Clearing House) [47] trap; I have seen so many update pages misfiled, and the volume ruined, because someone filed by the wrong numbers.

How often do you consult the documentation for services like Lexis or Westlaw?

Not very often. Even though Lexis and Westlaw like to brag that they have 11,000-plus databases, after a while you become so familiar with the sources that you know, like second nature, how they're updated, how often, and how current and inclusive they are.

How much search strategy planning goes on before logging on?

Very few of my staff sit down beforehand and formulate the query on paper. Years ago, I would have done that because the cost of *not* planning would have been prohibitive. It would have been a disservice to the client to do a search off the top of my head. I owed the client the duty of figuring out my strategy first, and making sure there were no holes in it. Now, with flat-fee arrangements, we have the ability to try a search one way and, if it doesn't work, not charge the client for that rabbit trail. I no longer encourage my staff to sit down and plot their strategies on the legal databases.

How do you usually build a search?

As a general rule, if it's an area of law that I know about, I start as narrowly as possible. If it's an area of law that I don't know about, I start as broadly as possible. It depends on my intimacy with the topic. That is probably how most of my staff would approach it. Because cost is not so much of an issue anymore, whichever way you have to expand the rubber band — either pull it out some more or let it in a little — you're not really impacting the client's bill.

What record format do you usually look at first to see if you are getting the right stuff?

KWIC (Key Word In Context) or whatever the equivalent of Lexis' KWIC might be, so the search words appear in context. I find that twenty-five words are enough. That helps you see, at least, how wonderful and how seductive words are. You think that particular combination of words couldn't possibly mean something else, yet within twenty-five words, you see that the myriad options are mind-boggling.

Text is more unruly than human nature.

You should bottle that quote.

If you are going to search either Lexis or Westlaw, when do you gravitate toward one or the other?

If it's something where we have a lot of confidence in the topic in the Key Number system, that gives Westlaw an edge right off the bat. There are not as many topics in which we *can* have confidence as West would like us to believe, but certain topics really are strong in West's system. They aren't garbage cans like Constitutional Law, or Appeal and Error, where anything that doesn't fit anywhere else has been thrown in.

What other online legal research services do you use?

Even though Lexis and Westlaw have legislative features, we have LEGI-SLATE [53], which we really love. It offers a lot more value in the way it makes the legislative history for you. Increasingly, if cost is a factor, and sometimes when time is a factor, we go to the court's Web site. We can find things more rapidly. There are resources on the Web that are not covered on Lexis or Westlaw, that have legal interest in specialty areas like communications law, food and drug law, or environmental law. We use those resources when they are better than Lexis and Westlaw in value-added features, completeness or currency.

What sort of value-added features?

Let's say they make the connections for you. Take an environmental database that includes the EPA [19] and all fifty states' codes, statutes and regulations. It is so much easier and less time-consuming to do a search that way and be able to link right away from the CD-ROM or the online database into the states you want. You can very quickly compare the state and the federal.

How much do you use CD-ROMs?

We were early adopters of CD-ROM and have basically made a commitment to abandon that technology. One reason is what's competing with it now: Publishers are providing the same information on the Net, and it's so much more current, and increasingly more retrospective. The second reason is that networking a CD-ROM with a site license of 400 is a complicated, human-resource-intensive effort for the IS folks. Believe it or not, it never became a plug-and-play technology.

When do you use the Internet for legal research?

We use the Internet if what we want is at a government site. At least for the primary source language and the material itself, it's far better to go to the government than to a commercial provider, even one with a good reputation like West or Lexis. If it's wrong and it's theirs, it's official. We also use the Internet if something is more current on the Net, and for certain things that are only available on the Net.

Doesn't that become a maddening mental matrix of currency and availability? Do you carry all that in your head?

You really do carry it in your head because, after a while — especially if you're the end user — you actually are restricting yourself to a limited universe of knowledge. The process is that you can rely on Lexis or whatever up to a certain point, but if you need to go further back or forward, you would need to verify it through the Net. In our constant education of the lawyers, we try to keep them apprised of that. I don't see it as a problem because completeness and currentness always have been the mountains lawyers have had to climb. Even in 1900, you had to have a way of getting to the law today. There was no excuse. You had to be complete and you had to be current.

In some cases would it be incompetent not to use the Internet?

In some cases it would be, if something were not as current in any other source. I don't know that there have been any cases on this, but I believe the courts would consider it a necessity.

Are there times you satisfy a legal research request using only the Internet?

There are a number of things that the government is making available — at least on a timely basis — only on the Internet. Heretofore, an agency like the FCC may have had a Public Affairs Office where they provided information on a same-day basis in paper. Now, because of various government initiatives, they've ceased doing that. So, often, you might find primary-source legal information only on the Net.

You find things on the Internet that you wouldn't find elsewhere. Much of that is what people might consider fringe literature, that can be very relevant to litigation. If a group of citizens who form a large class in class action litigation have created a home page to keep the class apprised of developments, this may be a wonderful way to find out what information is being disseminated to the class, particularly if you are representing the defendant.

You can find what some expert witness who's opposing you said in a newsgroup that could make him look silly in the courtroom.

Constantly. We do a lot of that. That is uniquely available on the Net. Somebody once told me that it's even more valuable than getting Q&A from scientific proceedings, because in the proceedings there's a guarded response. On the Net, there isn't. A person might say anything.

Do you use Lexis and Westlaw via their proprietary software or on the Web?

It depends. When people are on the road, they usually go through the Web. That's how we encourage them to do it. Here in the firm, we are hard-wired to both Lexis and Westlaw, so we use the proprietary software because it's instant. You are on Lexis or Westlaw by just pushing the icon. That's all you do on your end. You're already logged in and you come to this screen.

Are there things about the Web-based version of Westlaw or Lexis that you like better than the proprietary software?

No, but I think that's the "old-fashioned" in me. It seems to me that the staff also prefers the old-fashioned way for both systems. I think almost all the information vendors would agree that they have modeled the Web versions for the novice user. To be as hand-holding as possible, they clutter the screen with a lot of directional information. That's what we object to. If there were an option to get rid of all that clutter, that would make it much, much more user-friendly for us. Those "help" enhancements encourage and comfort the novice or insecure user, but they slow us down.

How do you find things on the Web?

We can usually intuit the name of the site we want to use. We do use search engines, just not as often, perhaps, as a nonprofessional researcher would. We use FindLaw [6] quite a bit. This is not necessarily a good idea, but searchers tend to develop a group of favorite Web search engines, maybe four or five, mostly for personal reasons. As new ones come along, I tend not to try them out until I exhaust my current five; then I think, "Oh you know, Tom really likes that one, maybe I'll try it." We have not had as much comfort or success with metasearch engines as they've been touted as providing.

Do you use Internet resources that are not on the Web?

We use telnet to go to OPACs (online public access catalogs), particularly non-U.S. library sources. We use OCLC [98] a lot to find materials for interlibrary loan, although, if it's a non-U.S. source, it might not be included in OCLC.

Do you use listservs and newsgroups?

Oh yes. We monitor them for library and librarianship issues. We throw out a "How do you do this?" or "How do you handle this?" question at least once a week. It's a wonderful way to gather industry practice very, very quickly. Some of the librarians on the staff are involved in chat groups. They set aside a certain time of day to chat with experts. They consider that a form of continuing education.

How do you keep current with new legal resources coming onto the Internet?

It's hard, because it's such an organic thing. It's constantly growing and changing. We have one librarian who actually specializes in the Internet. That is her whole function, to monitor the Net for the entire firm — not that others of us aren't doing that constantly, too. She also is responsible for making sure all the linkages are still good within the firm's intranet, and for adding new ones. I, like the lawyers in the firm, depend on another person to filter the Net for me.

On the firm's intranet, do you have a page of links to sites for which you might not intuit the uniform resource locator (URL)?

Yes. It's immensely extensive. All the government sites we use are there. We try to include all of our clients' home pages so that you can immediately link to them. We have hundreds of clients. We have links to trade associations that represent our clients. We have links to international sites that, due to geography, might be unique on the Net. We'll add the sites of opposing counsel or co-counsel to our list. It's enormous.

Once you leave "dot gov," how do you feel about the quality of Internet information?

It varies, especially the trade association information. Some trade association sites are just PR and not really informational. You can't take their industry statistics to be true.

What are the main deficiencies of Internet legal resources?

If you had asked me that question two years ago, I would have said there wasn't enough federal government information, or that what was there was not complete. Increasingly, the government has stepped up to the plate, and it gets better every day. It's more comprehensive, more retrospective, more current, and more endemic. I am very much sold on the Web, but it does have to do with the fact that my key access is, as you say, "dot gov."

Has there been a search where you felt sure the information had to be on the Web but you never found it?

The first president of the Smithsonian Institution was named something like R. David O'Donnell. I don't remember why, but we needed to know what the R. stood for. It might be out there, but I gave up on the Web before I found it.

Do you find yourself explaining the deficiencies of Internet research to the people who request information from you?

I used to. Two years ago I would say to people, "It's not complete, it's not verifiable, it's coming from possibly bootleg sources, so you don't want to use it." One time we were looking for the enacted version of the North American Free Trade Agreement (NAFTA). We found it on the Net, but we found it in eleven different places with seven different, easily discernible versions. We couldn't tell which was the veritable source. There wasn't a government source on the Web at the time. We found that half or more of those sites were just somebody who mooshed together, for lack of a better word, different pieces of different sections and put it up as NAFTA.

How do you handle data from the Internet? Are you doing a lot of File Save As or are you using some other software to deal with it?

For now, we use File Save As, and we have to remember to save the graphics. We create a new folder in Windows and save all the work for a project to that folder. When we start the next project, we create another folder and save it all there. Very cumbersome. There are five or six steps to it. We were just saying, the other day, that we have to find a better solution. We are on the prowl for it now. Around here, when you notice a technology problem, you identify it for the IS people. They will see if they can buy something off the shelf to solve it, or if they need to write a customized program. We haven't found it yet. The firm might have to create it.

What would you want such a program to do?

I would like to see the results of searching go into an internal intelligence bank automatically. You have all kinds of data structure decisions to make. I would like it to emulate our work product files and our intellectual capital files. The goal of the firm is to make searching — and this is a trade name but we use it as a generic term here — *uniface*. Hopefully we could do that with Web output.

How long do you save your search results?

For as long as the file needs to be open. It could be years. In the future I may send it to a firm archive and not keep it on an active drive.

Do you find yourself bookmarking sites for fear you wouldn't find them again?

In the beginning, constantly. Devices like bookmarking were necessary. Not now. After a while you reach a comfort level; a site is going to be there and the site name becomes second nature to you, like you know all the phone numbers that you can rattle off.

How has the Internet affected the role of the professional legal researcher?

It's two-fold. Just last year, our staff was twenty-six people. The majority of those people were non-librarians, support staff. Now we have lost three people; we've downsized. They were all from the support staff side. We keep increasing the number of librarians. That's because, not just the Net, but the whole world in which we live, the entire information environment, requires some kind of intermediary to serve the end-user in a profit-making environment.

In library science jargon, it's called customization and disintervention. That means the professional librarian has two roles now. Customization means the professional legal researcher has the role of doing customized research. That means being able to find information that is not commonly known, even to an expert, the real needle in a haystack that will be the turning point of the case. Because that process involves navigating through so many different formats, *you're* the one who has to find that needle.

You also have to enable the user to be free to do work without you. That's disintervention. To do that, you have to set up a false freedom for them: You have to get them some control over the information universe. You can see disintervention in our training program and very, very much in our intranet site. You have to select for the user, predict, be proactive and know how to refine what they will need to know. If they can't find what they need in the disintervention part, the free part, you have to be waiting in the wings, in the customization part, to find it for them.

Do you have a favorite Internet search story you like to tell?

Our client was going to invest in a country of the former Soviet Union. We found a site that described plans for the country's banking system, and conveyed the information to our client. That bit of information enabled them to cut a better deal. If we hadn't gone on the Net, we never would have known that information existed.

What can a person who is requesting research do to help you do the best job?

If they know what they want, they have the duty to present the information to us in the clearest format. In fact, if they don't know what they want, it's important to actually come right out and say, "I am on a fishing expedition. I have these intuitions about what I want, that there might be something on it, or that this could have been mentioned somewhere, but I really don't know." What's frustrating and wastes time is when someone appears confident saying, "I saw it in *The New York Times* [85] last week" and, as it turns out, it was in *The Wall Street Journal* two years ago. If they admit they don't remember which paper it was, you could do a search in *The Washington Post* [86], *The New York Times,* and whatever else they usually read, and in five minutes cover all of them.

You'd rather have them tell you more than less, even if you're not sure you need it.

Exactly. We don't mind reading long search requests because, invariably, that helps make short research. The more information we get, the shorter the request actually is. We've studied that.

What do you love about searching?

Unlike a lot of my colleagues, I don't really like the challenge, the means, but I love the end. What I love about being a librarian is that you are exposed to so much more knowledge than you would be in any other profession. This is true even if you're a law librarian or some other kind of special librarian. You learn so much. No matter how difficult the getting there, at the end you have the incredible reward of the find.

What is most attractive to you about doing research online?

The speed at which you can do it. The immediate feedback of the answer and the ability to evaluate it. Being liberated. Having the choice between looking at something using someone else's taxonomy, like an indexer or a West Key Number system, versus letting your own mind create the taxonomy. With the books, you don't have the freedom to think of it the way *you* think of it. You're constrained by how somebody else chose to present it.

Super Searcher Secrets

- *On working around the lack of a reference interview in an email world...*If you are involved in the early phases of a lawyer's orientation at the firm, you can explain the kinds of things that are important to know in a research request and the kinds of omissions that will totally skew the response. The reference interview then becomes less important. There's always going to be some ambiguity. We can find the ambiguity by doing a little bit of research and getting back to them. The second contact is richer.
- *On alternatives to checklists and pathfinders...*When people come to work for us, we try to have them in a "shadow" situation for several months. They watch the other librarians, learning how things are done here, and learning about the pitfalls in research.
- *On the raison d'être of citators...*We often tell the lawyers that the *raison d'être* of KeyCite and Shepard's is as a research tool as well as a source validation tool. We would be hard-pressed to tell them which function is more important.
- *On what affects the entry point of research...*Some areas of law have developed on legal principles and other areas are driven by facts. If the question is a fact-based one, nine

times out of ten I tell a researcher, at any level of expertise, to go online and do a keyword search with the facts as well-articulated as they can be. If it's an area of law building on legal principles, we often keep them in the treatises and the law review articles, which tend not to be fact-based so much as legal principle-based.

- *On what to use the Internet for...*We use the Internet if what we want is at a government site. At least for the primary source language and material itself, it's far better to go to the government than to a commercial provider, even one with a good reputation like West or Lexis. If it's wrong and it's theirs, it's official. We also use the Internet if something is more current on the Net, and for certain things that are only available on the Net.

- *On what can only be done on the Internet...*You find things on the Internet that you wouldn't find elsewhere. Much of that is what people might consider fringe literature, that can be very relevant to litigation. If a group of citizens who form a large class in class action litigation have created a home page to keep the class apprised of developments, this may be a wonderful way to find out what information is being disseminated to the class, particularly if you are representing the defendant.

- *On preference of proprietary or Web access to commercial services...*I think almost all the information vendors would agree that they have modeled the Web versions for the novice user. To be as hand-holding as possible, they clutter the screen with a lot of directional information. That's what we object to. If there were an option to get rid of all that clutter, that would make it much, much more user-friendly for us.

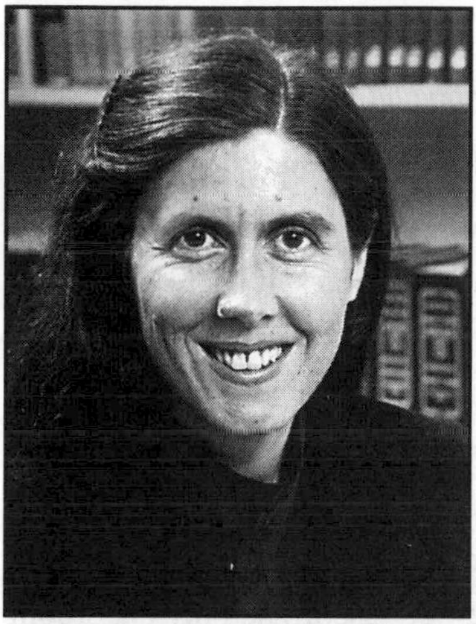

Catherine P. Best

Not Getting Lost in What You Find

Catherine P. Best is a research lawyer with the Vancouver, BC firm of Campney & Murphy and author of the *Best Guide to Canadian Legal Research*. Ms. Best is adjunct professor in Legal Research, Faculty of Law, University of British Columbia. She has practiced as a research lawyer in a wide variety of subject areas since 1987, including insurance, corporations, torts, contracts, administrative law, employment, Crown liability, securities, property, constitutional law, intellectual property, insolvency, evidentiary and practice issues, banking, trusts and estates, maritime law, and environmental law. She researches and analyzes the law, writes legal opinions and memoranda, and prepares legal arguments for court and other types of hearings. *Any statements, representations, inferences, or impressions are those of Catherine P. Best and do not reflect upon the practices, policies, or opinions of Campney & Murphy.*

cpbest@interchange.ubc.ca
legalresearch.org

How did you get into legal research?

I have always enjoyed doing research. After I finished law school, I clerked for six judges on the Supreme Court of British Columbia for a year. Then I went to a general corporate commercial practice in a large firm that was quite demanding. After a few years, I wanted something more flexible where I wouldn't have such crazy hours. I decided to change to a research practice and found a firm willing to hire me to do that. Since then my practice has been exclusively legal research. Occasionally I go to court and junior on an appeal when I have written the argument. I also spent two years at the University of British Columbia Faculty of Law directing their legal research and writing program.

Tell me about your Web site, *Best Guide to Canadian Legal Research* [2, see Appendix A]. How did that get started?

For several years I taught an advanced legal research course at UBC with a limited number of third year students. It was a very high-quality course and was considered a Cadillac because of the amount of energy and resources it took to deliver. There were many more upper level students who wanted to take research training, so I tried to figure out a way to deliver a less resource-intensive course to more people. I decided to explore Internet delivery, and taught two sections of the advanced course that were Internet-based. The only classroom time was one hands-on tutorial a week. Each student had to complete a number of short assignments and a research paper using the skills taught in the course. Course readings were partially in print and partially electronic. Students posted some of their short assignments on the course discussion list, and posted comments on the various approaches that could be taken to the research task. The emphasis was on critically approaching the material and finding efficient and effective ways to use the research tools.

The electronic readings were largely a re-working of teaching material I had been using for several years. Those readings underwent another major revision for the *Best Guide to Canadian Legal Research*. In addition, I included the tutorial scripts used for teaching the students how to use electronic research tools. I have put this material up on the Internet hoping it will encourage lawyers and students to learn that their research can be improved if they follow a process, at least initially, instead of approaching it haphazardly. For so many people, it seems, electronic research is a bit of a mystery. The tutorial scripts on the Web site will walk someone through the main commands and features of a particular electronic research tool within an hour and a half.

At the firm, how do your research requests come to you?

Usually a lawyer calls me up and says they have a project they'd like me to work on. Sometimes I just get a memo or an email message.

Sometimes they walk into my office. Occasionally, when I've had a close relationship with a large client who requires frequent opinion work, I get assignments from them directly by either fax or email. There is still some reluctance to use email because of the confidential nature of the material.

Do you have an intake procedure for new research requests?

Most of my research assignments come directly from the lawyers in my firm. I find out the file number so I have something to bill my time and disbursements to. I get some idea of the budget for the project, the time line, and the format they prefer for the material they'll receive. Often, they come to me with a fair amount of detail about what they want. Sometimes I just get a very generic description of the problem and a file number, and the lawyer omits to tell me important things like which party we're acting for. I find it helpful to know whom we are representing: It shapes the way I approach the research and the kind of answer I'd like to be able to give. It also makes a difference if I'm being asked to give a very objective assessment of the law, as opposed to preparing an argument using an advocacy approach. The preferable situation is where we sit down and talk about the assignment and make sure I understand fully what the lawyer wants.

Does being a research lawyer involve you in helping to formulate the statement of the issues?

We work on them together. Sometimes, when the project comes to me, it hasn't been broken down into legal issues yet. It's a bunch of facts that need to be worked with. Often, the issues are highly defined. It varies from one project to the next. Sometimes, after I've taken a look at it, I go back to the lawyer and say, "That's one way we could approach it, but there are these other ways of looking at it."

Has the Internet had any effect on that initial stage?

No, but it will, once we get a significant number of research memoranda and other documents into an in-house electronic database. We are currently designing a research database that we can use through our firm's intranet. Once that is operational, one of the first things I would do is look there to see what we already have. Hopefully it will be user-friendly enough that the lawyers in the office will use it, too, and will look there before they even come to see me.

How quickly do you turn around your projects?

There is a huge variation. Sometimes there is a call from the courthouse during the morning break, when something is needed before they go back at two o'clock. It doesn't happen a lot, but it can. Sometimes the research is needed sixty days down the road.

What kind of product do you deliver?

I usually write a well-reasoned memo drawn from the authorities. Sometimes the budget or the time line doesn't permit that, and I make just an oral report with copies of the cases. More often than not, I do write a memorandum. Sometimes I write the documents for court. I'll write a brief or a factum about thirty percent of the time. A factum in Canadian practice is the written argument put before an appellate level court.

Your Web site has a fabulous set of pages called "Plan and Organize Your Research." You do emphasize that one can't always follow a sequence in a linear fashion, and that there may be things outside the sequence that a person should think about creatively. That said, in actual practice are you usually able to follow the sequence?

As a general rule, I tend to start with a secondary source, move into primary sources, and then do updating. I follow that pattern pretty regularly in most assignments, but every project is different. There are ones where I've been given some cases already, or I have a memo that gives me a head start. If I'm starting with a statute, often I go right to an annotated version of the statute. I may then go to a secondary source that deals with the statute to give me some context, and I will look at cases listed in the annotation. I may look at cases that consider statutes with similar language from other jurisdictions.

How does your previous familiarity with a particular area of law affect the way you start a project?

It determines how much I look in secondary sources before I get down into primary sources. Even if I have a general familiarity with the subject, looking in secondary sources is still really valuable. It tends to highlight where the grey areas are. It suggests approaches or ways to analyze the material where the case law isn't clear. It highlights additional things to think about that might not occur to me on my own.

Are you sometimes asked to "get me everything on" a certain subject?

That used to happen more than it does now. Clients have become extremely concerned about cost, and the firm has become concerned as a result. It's less often that I get a leave-no-stone-unturned or exhaustive survey request. Those take a very long time.

Do you normally run a search straight through, or is there an iterative process where, during the intermediate stages, you converse again with the lawyer to see if you're heading the right way?

It varies from project to project. In retrospect, usually I wish I had talked with the lawyer more as I was doing the project. Sometimes we have a conversation because we run into each other in the hall, and I discover information or feedback that would have been useful a couple of days earlier. I was working on something recently that had quite a complex set of facts, and I wanted to be sure I had them right. I emailed the lawyer a draft of what I had written to date, to make sure I was on track. It was really important to focus the memo. It's crucial to keep that dialogue going. Students and junior lawyers are often reluctant to approach the lawyer for clarification if they are unsure about something. It is preferable to ask the question than to spend several hours, or even days, going down the wrong path.

How do you document where and how you've searched?

I keep copious notes. Every time I open a book, I write down the name, author, year, and usually the publisher. For loose-leaf books, I always write down the date of the most recent release I've checked. When I look in digests, I write down the headings I've looked under. When I do computer searches, I write down my search string, the databases I went into, and the date.

I have a feeling that, in many firms, a lot of things are done over for lack of proper notes and doubt about what had already been done.

I think that's right. If a question ever came up about the extent of the research done, my notes would enable me to state with confidence what had been reviewed. However, the form in which I keep my notes means they are not necessarily useful for others. They are in the file, in my handwriting, and they go back to the lawyer with the rest of the research documents. A more useful research bibliography containing this type of information would be typewritten and appended to each research memorandum. Unfortunately, the time pressures and costs of research in private practice make this type of research bibliography more the exception than the rule.

Do you file your notes so that, if the case file comes back, you could readily find your notes for it?

Yes. I keep a fairly structured file while I'm working on anything. I always have a brown accordion folder with inside sub-folders, and I'll have a different one for each issue. For some projects I might have six or seven issues. If I keep it all in one pile, it just gets jumbled. I always have a folder called "Notes" for my research strategy and research bibliography notes. It's never that fat, and this material is always accessible in that file. When I first get the project and map out my initial strategy for where I want to look, I put the strategy in that folder. I add to this as I refine my research strategy. I keep a rough outline of the issues I am researching, and flesh it out as I go with sub-issues. As I proceed, I include notes on which cases and statutes I've updated, and notes for every source I've looked at. I put material specific to a discrete issue into the subfolder for that issue, and cross-reference material that relates to more than one issue. I've watched people struggle with being able to write, once they've done the research. They may get through the research okay, but then they have a pile of stuff they can't deal with for writing. They have to go back to the process of separating out the issues and figuring out what relates to what. The same case may relate to three discrete issues. You have to be organized mentally to get from a tangle of concepts to structured, well-reasoned analysis. Organizing your research papers helps that process.

How does budget affect the way you research?

For me, budget affects everything. It affects how much time I can spend and how much online research can be done. Both have quite significant costs. My time is charged back to the client, and I've been doing this long enough that my time is expensive. I am constantly making strategic decisions based on budget considerations: Is it worth my going to the hardcopy, or is it more efficient, economically, for me to do this online if it will take less time? It's a trade-off between the cost of my time and the cost of the disbursements. When updating a case, how many of the citing cases should I be checking, and how should I decide which ones to review? Another trade-off is the one between being comprehensive and being efficient. How long should I spend continuing to look for that elusive perfect case? This is a matter of judgment that improves with experience and familiarity with the sources, but it is also budget-driven. I often ask if there is a limit on how much time the lawyer wants spent on the file. Sometimes I am told not to spend more than three hours, which is very little time. Sometimes I'm told to do what I have to do to answer the question, because it is really important.

Between those two extremes, are you ever asked to estimate the cost of doing the research the way you would like to do it?

I'm not often asked how many hours I think it will take. The more usual scenario is that the lawyer tells me my time limit. Sometimes I will be asked to contribute to a client proposal containing an estimate of what it would cost to do the research. It's very difficult to estimate in advance how long legal research is going to take, but it is often necessary in order to attract the work. If you've given an estimate, then you just do the work as efficiently as you can to meet the budget you've set. Sometimes you can't do it. When I'm working under what I consider to be a very constrained budget, I make that clear in the written work I give out. I mention that the results are limited by the time allotted and that I normally would have checked certain other sources, but was not able to. I make it clear where I've had to cut corners if I'm not comfortable with the final product.

We should develop some disclaimers or reminders of the parameters when we give our product.

Certainly, because otherwise the reader has no idea whether the research memorandum was the result of limited or comprehensive research. Without this information, people become reluctant to include their memoranda in a research database. They worry that someone else might use it without being aware of the constraints under which the work was performed. If we were all disciplined enough to include a research bibliography with each project, it could serve this purpose. The projects with tight time constraints are precisely the type of projects where the researcher usually doesn't have time to prepare a research bibliography. So, some type of statement located in a prominent part of the document should be included to indicate that the researcher did not look at certain types of sources. For example, "In the limited time allotted for this assignment, I was unable to review the Ontario cases on this point. Please advise if you would like me to do further research in this area."

What CD-ROM products do you find useful?

Our statutes are on CD-ROM, both the federal and provincial ones. The CD-ROM versions of the statutes tend to be considerably more up-to-date than the consolidated versions on the Internet. Once a law firm has purchased the CD-ROM, it's more cost-effective to use than the commercial databases, but the CD-ROM is usually not as current as the commercial databases. We have some full-text periodical material on CD-ROM, as well as case digest collections, and products focusing on specific areas of practice, such as tax and securities. You can do a fair amount of Canadian research on CD-ROM, but the products are expensive. When the firm buys CD-ROM products, they are an overhead expense, the cost of which is included in the firm's hourly rates in the same way as other library resources. If I use an online commercial database, it's charged to the client as a disbursement. As the lines become blurred, with the introduction of flat-rate pricing for online research and the ability to track CD-ROM usage for billing purposes, this distinction between how these various electronic research tools are billed might fade away.

What factors trigger the need for electronic research?

The first factor is availability. Although we have a good library at our firm, there are lots of things we don't have. I weigh the cost of going to another library to look at material versus dialing up to get it. If I can be really efficient, it's usually cheaper for me to dial up and do it electronically. For example, ordering photocopied cases from another library usually costs about fifty cents per page, plus a courier charge. There is a time lag of at least a few hours until the order arrives. I often can download a case for considerably less than that. Often I need to look at material from other jurisdictions that is not available at our libraries. Even the larger research libraries have cut back on print resources in favor of electronic research tools. The second factor is that electronic research affords a different way to approach the material: It provides random access instead of relying on indexes. I can find things electronically that would not be located in a print search. The third factor is currency. The most current material is usually only available online. The fourth factor is efficiency. Often, I can find information much faster by researching electronically.

How deep is the back file of case law on QuickLaw?

QuickLaw [58] is the leading commercial online service for Canadian legal research. The full-text case law in many QL databases starts in 1986, although QL is gradually adding older cases, and some case databases have considerably more historical depth, such as the Supreme Court of Canada [39] database. There are also case digest databases that go back much further. I often search the digests electronically and get references to cases, the full text of which I can find in print. The lack of historical depth on QL has been a serious limitation for conducting comprehensive Canadian research online. Carswell [36] has just introduced a competing online research service that does contain older Canadian case law, and QL is now feeling some competitive pressure to add the older case law. Those with access to both services should be able to conduct fairly comprehensive Canadian case law research online. The cost of online research means that a researcher usually doesn't have that luxury. I think it is best to use a combination of print and electronic sources. I would rarely, if ever, complete a research project using electronic sources only.

Aside from the shallow back file of full-text cases, is there a hardcopy resource for which there is, as yet, no good online substitute?

The leading Canadian case digest collection, the *Canadian Abridgment*, is available electronically in a number of formats, and the *Canadian Encyclopedic Digest* is available in CD-ROM. Most secondary sources are only available in print. With the exception of some works that are published as part of a topical CD-ROM product, treatises and textbooks are only available in hardcopy. Many Canadian legal periodicals are also published only in print, although more are becoming available electronically.

What is your preferred method of checking whether a case is still good law? I think you use the term "noting up" for that in Canadian practice.

I usually update cases electronically, unless I'm told there is no budget for online research. I keep the cost to a minimum by printing out the results and following up the references using print sources. There are two comprehensive services for updating Canadian cases. Carswell publishes Canadian Case Citations as part of the *Canadian Abridgment*. It is available in print and in electronic format. QuickLaw has its own proprietary citator called QuickCite. I tell my students that it's a good idea to look at both of them, because you can get quite different results. In practice, it is hard to follow this rule because of both time and cost constraints.

What is your preferred method of finding cases that construe a statute or a regulation?

My preferred method is to start with an annotated version of the statute. If there is a text dealing with the subject area, I look at it as well. Another source for quickly finding judicial consideration of statutes is the *Canadian Encyclopedic Digest*. After this, I usually go to the statutes judicially considered sources. Of these, I start with the ones that provide a short summary of the case. My next step is to check my results against the Canadian Statute Citations, published as part of the *Canadian Abridgment*. This is a comprehensive citator that simply lists the names of cases considering the statutory provision. It is available in both print and electronic formats. For the most current judicial consideration, I search in the full-text case law databases on QL for references to the statutory provision.

Aside from QuickLaw, CD-ROMs and the Internet, what other online sources do you have for Canadian legal research?

Carswell has just introduced several online products available by subscription on the Internet, called eCarswell. The *law.pro* product contains the *Abridgment* case digests and citators as well as an extensive collection of full-text Canadian cases. Unlike the ongoing competition between Lexis [54] and Westlaw [60] in the United States, QuickLaw has not had a major competitor until now. It will be interesting to see whether the market is receptive to the Carswell product, and to see how QuickLaw responds to this initiative. Although Lexis carries some Canadian legal materials, its coverage is not broad, so I rarely use it for Canadian legal research. I do use it for certain publications that are only available on Lexis, such as the *Lawyers Weekly*.

Some U.S. states have their own online legal research services. In Montana we have a fairly decent one called MontLaw. In Canada, are there some smaller, maybe provincial level, online legal search services?

There are some. Quebec case law is available through an online service called SOQUIJ [38]. Maritime Law Books publishes several case reporters that are available on a subscription-based Web site, as well as on Lexis. Western Legal Publications, which publishes case digests from the four western provinces, has created a number of CD-ROM products that are widely available. The federal and provincial governments have published the statutes and regulations in both CD-ROM format and on the Internet. The federal government has gotten into electronic publishing in a big way for statutes and regulations, to the point where print consolidations of the federal statutes and regulations are no longer being published between revisions. The most recent print consolidation of the federal statutes is only current to April 1993, and the most recent print consolidation of the federal regulations was published in 1978!

How much planning do you do before logging on to QuickLaw?

I do a fair amount. I always make a list of keywords, synonyms and alternate words, and think about which words should be truncated. I think about what databases to search and make a note of them. Then, as I do the search, I refine it and check off what I've searched. Depending on how complex the search is and how many alternate terms it includes, my search plan is more like a diagram, with several columns of alternate terms separated by the appropriate connectors.

On QuickLaw, are you able to expressly control the order of operation of the connectors, such as by nesting with parentheses?

You cannot use parentheses on QuickLaw. You have to understand the order in which the operators are evaluated. It's very confusing even to people who use QuickLaw regularly. QuickLaw has two different forms of OR. A space between two words is an implicit OR, just as it is on Westlaw. If you use an explicit OR on QuickLaw it performs a different function than the implicit OR does. On Westlaw, it doesn't matter whether you type out the word or insert a space, it's evaluated the same way. Although QuickLaw doesn't permit the use of parentheses, effective use of these two different commands for OR can overcome this limitation. Assume that I want to conduct a search for cases dealing with punitive or aggravated damages in the areas of libel or slander. A good search query would be *punitive aggravated /5 damages AND libel slander defamation*. What if I have two entirely different concepts that I want to separate? For example, I want to find out whether an arbitrator has jurisdiction to grant equitable remedies such as specific performance or an injunction. In this case, a good search query would be *"specific performance" OR injunction AND arbitrator /P jurisdiction*. The main distinction is that the implicit OR takes precedence over proximity commands, while the explicit OR does not. In Westlaw, by distinction, OR always takes precedence over proximity commands whether implicit or explicit.

Does OR precede AND on QuickLaw?

Yes, regardless of whether you use the implicit or explicit OR. The order of precedence on QuickLaw is, from left to right: terms in quotation marks, implicit OR, proximity connectors (from left to right), explicit OR, AND, and BUT NOT. Because you can't use parentheses to force the order in which your terms will be evaluated on QuickLaw, it is very important that you understand the order of precedence. Also, you should not assume that all search engines use the same order of precedence or even the same commands. I can remember the first time I used Lexis, how blown away I was when nothing was coming up the way I expected it to. Then I realized that Lexis treats a space between two words as a phrase and not as an OR. To make things even more confusing for the average Canadian researcher, FolioViews treats a space as an AND! These are fundamental differences and lead into concerns I have about effective searching on the Internet. I don't think most people have a clue what happens to the words they type into those little boxes on the screen. I'm not talking about people who do this for a living or use it all the time, but the average user who just plunks some words in there. Because of relevancy ranking, some of the documents search engines retrieve are quite relevant. For me, that's not good enough. I need to know that I have retrieved everything that's highly relevant to what I'm doing. I don't know how you can ever be sure of that if you don't know how the search engine works.

How often do you consult the documentation for a search service while planning your search strategy?

For Lexis, Westlaw, QuickLaw, and the FolioViews CD-ROM products, I'm very familiar with their syntax. I don't need to look that up anymore. Particularly for Westlaw and Lexis, I often find it useful to look at their database lists to make sure I'm using the most effective database. When I go on the Internet, I do need to check the syntax. For the specifically legal search tools on the Internet, I've made myself a chart. The first time I use an Internet search tool, I take a good look at the search syntax and I make a chart. What's AND on this site? What proximity options do I have? How do I do OR? How can I refine a search? I have a chart like this on my Web site that covers the major Canadian legal Internet sites. Before I do a search I usually look at it, because each site is different and I can't remember it all. I've actually printed that one out and stuck it up on my bulletin board.

I try never to use things like +'s and -'s where words are available, because I can remember words.

That's right, if you can use AND or OR, it's better. Sometimes you have to capitalize the connectors and sometimes they don't accept phrase searches. On some search engines, /5 is an ordered proximity search for two words within five of each other, while on others, /5 is an unordered proximity search. Some automatically search for plurals and truncations and some don't. There are so many different search engines in regular use now that it's next to impossible to remember them, and yet it's so crucial to your search results that you use them properly.

Let's talk about file selection on the commercial services.

My first step usually is to search digests if I can, rather than going straight to full text. I search on small summaries of the cases, in files with fairly comprehensive coverage. For searching in the States, I tend to go to Westlaw first and search in the synopsis and digest fields, rather than the full text of the database. To test those results I might search again using natural language in full text, and compare the search results.

For full-text searching, do you gravitate more toward natural language or Boolean searching?

When I'm using Westlaw and Lexis, I often check both, but I prefer the Westlaw natural language search engine to the Lexis Freestyle. I get better results more consistently. I trust Westlaw more and would tend to run Westlaw searches using both approaches. I also try to take advantage of the value-added material on Westlaw. I often conduct manual research to find the Key Numbers that are most appropriate, and then do Key Number searches electronically, in association with distinctive search terms. I seldom just go out there and do a wide open full-text search. An exception is periodicals research. I have had good success with natural language searches in the full-text periodicals databases, and sometimes it is a good starting point.

How do you usually build a search?

In hardcopy research, I often start quite broad, by looking at textbooks. In online research, I definitely start narrow, looking for something that's very particular, very much on my subject. Sometimes, bingo — it's right there! I might find, on the first search, something that's directly on point. Then I start noting up relevant cases and reading the internal references within. On most projects, I work from both ends, starting more broadly in textbooks to get a conceptual context and references to leading cases, and searching narrowly online, looking for cases that are specifically on my fact pattern. The broader conceptual research is important. It helps me build my research vocabulary, alerts me to controversial or uncertain areas, provides a policy framework, and helps me understand how various legal doctrines interact in my subject area. It ensures that I am not approaching the online research too narrowly.

Since you work from both ends, you are able to confirm whether you started your online search too narrowly.

That's right. Confirmation also comes by doing other things, such as noting up the cases I come across, and reading other cases referred to in the secondary sources. I often reverse-engineer things. Say I come across a case that I didn't find one way. I'll look for the case to see how it was indexed in the other sources; perhaps I missed some relevant keywords or classifications in the course of my research. That will lead me into other material. It's very much a back-and-forth process among sources.

Even when you start narrow in an electronic search, do you sometimes find yourself getting too much stuff?

Only when the terms are very generic. If I am able to use quite distinctive terms, it's often fairly successful. Sometimes the words are used in ways you don't expect, and you get a lot of irrelevant material. I'm experienced enough to say, "This isn't going to work on the computer." One way to narrow a search where the terms are too generic is to find the relevant *Abridgment* classification, and then search within the case digests using that classification with the addition of a few keywords. This would be similar to including a Key Number in a Westlaw search query. It is a good technique for increasing relevancy when your search terms are too generic.

Because you usually start off in the digest, you're able to see easily whether you are getting the right stuff, because the digest paragraphs are relatively short. When you are searching full text, what record format do you look at first?

If the case has a headnote, I quickly scan it first. A headnote in a Canadian case is roughly equivalent to the synopsis and digest in U.S. cases. On QuickLaw, I can use the Locate command to go to screens where my search terms appear. This is similar to Term Locate mode in Westlaw, but the Locate command must be entered each time you change screens.

Does QuickLaw have a KWIC format?

QuickLaw has no command similar to KWIC on Lexis, which gives you a limited display of twenty-five words on either side of your search terms. The new Carswell product, *law.pro*, gives you a two- to three-line summary of each case on the hit list, based on the first part of the case digest. This can be helpful in deciding whether to review the case, but often it doesn't contain enough information to enable one to make this decision.

When you're on Lexis, then, do you like to use KWIC?

I do use it. However, the size is often too small for me to evaluate properly the relevancy of the case. I usually expand it to fifty words on either side rather than twenty-five, using VAR KWIC (Variable Key Word In Context). Another advantage of VAR KWIC is that, when you switch to FULL display, you are more likely to get to the part of the document you want to be in. With KWIC, I often find that, when I switch to FULL, I end up in the next section of the document rather than the section I wanted to see. If I use VAR KWIC I can avoid that problem.

If you are going to search either Lexis or Westlaw, when do you gravitate toward Westlaw and when toward Lexis?

For American research, I prefer using Westlaw. Besides preferring its natural language search engine, I like the West value-addeds, like the synopsis and the Key Numbers. I prefer KeyCite in some respects to the Shepard's citator on Lexis, although there are some drawbacks to the KeyCite service. On the other hand, the hourly rate for using Westlaw is much higher in Canada than the rate Lexis charges Canadians for American research. Most Canadian users pay hourly rates for these two services, not a flat rate, so cost is a big factor in choosing which service to use. If I only need to pull a case off, it makes more sense to do that from Lexis. I use Lexis extensively for English research. Westlaw doesn't have that material.

Do you use databases like LegalTrac?

Yes. I don't know how many private law firms have LegalTrac, but it is used very heavily at the university. In private practice, this material is often accessed through the LRI databases on Westlaw and Lexis. The main databases used at the university for legal periodicals research are LegalTrac and the Index to Legal Periodicals. However, there is also a Canadian legal periodicals index published in print and electronic format, called *Index to Canadian Legal Literature*. When I was on the faculty at UBC I used periodical articles considerably more than I do in private practice. They are still an extremely useful resource for finding references to relevant sources, explaining the policy behind the law, and coming up with new approaches to difficult issues.

With CD-ROMs, do you have to use a lot of different software?

Most of them use FolioViews. The search syntax doesn't change from one FolioViews product to another, but the products differ in what is designated as a record and what enhancements have been added. In the default query screen, a record is one paragraph. This means that all your search terms must occur within one paragraph in order to retrieve the document. If you are searching a statute, each sub-section, rather than each section, will be a separate record.

Do you have cases on CD-ROM?

Yes, and this is where the publishers have had to be a little more creative. If they just do the bare bones Folio development with each paragraph being a separate record, you're not able to search effectively on the full text. They have had to build templates and push the product so that it is effective for that kind of research.

Do you encounter data quality problems with the commercial database services?

A lot of the material on QuickLaw comes directly from the courts in electronic format. The quality of the data depends on the judge's secretary who typed it up. It's the same with material the courts are putting on the Internet. If the material has already gone through an editing process to be published in a reporter, it tends to be pretty good. If the material has gone directly from the courts to QuickLaw, it is more likely to have typographical errors, although that has vastly improved over the years.

What factors lead you to use the Internet to research a point of law?

Sometimes it's a cost factor. Our British Columbia court has had its own Internet site since August 1996. It has all the BC case law since then. Every day they put up the new case law. It's a wonderful resource. Sometimes I pull off a copy of the case there, rather than pay to get it somewhere else. It does have a search engine. It's not as sophisticated as the ones on the commercial services, but it works. The Supreme Court of Canada decisions from 1989 are up on a site [40]. I tend to go to those sites just to download cases, not to run searches. I will run searches sometimes, but I still don't trust that I've gotten everything, and I'm cautious. Sometimes I'll know that the Supreme Court of Canada made a decision on a certain issue, but I won't have the name or the cite. In that instance, I'll run a search and download the case. It has worked fairly well, but there's not a huge volume of material there.

There are some emerging areas of law where the Internet should be searched, such as computer law, cyberlaw, and Y2K issues. Print sources on these topics tend to be outdated before they are even published. Some Canadian administrative tribunals are publishing their decisions on the Internet rather than through a commercial online service, which makes the Internet the best vehicle for researching their decisions. The European and international law resources available on the Internet are very good, and often surpass what is available in local libraries. So, despite my general lack of enthusiasm for Internet research, there are some research tasks where it may be the best place to go.

How does the Internet fit into your overall research approach?

I view it as one of many tools I can use. I might use it when I'm concerned about cost, although it usually takes longer to do things using the Internet. The cost of my time is a factor, so it may not be more cost-effective. It's pretty much restricted to when I know there is a case. Let's say I do some research on QuickLaw and there are five recent BC decisions that I should be looking at. Rather than download those from QuickLaw, I'll go to the BC Superior Courts site [34, 35] and pull off the cases. I definitely use the Internet to go to government sites to look at bills that have been introduced recently. I can get them on the Internet while they are still under deliberation, or right after they have been enacted, while the other services lag in getting them up.

Are there times when failure to use the Internet might be considered incompetent? That's a strong word, isn't it?

Yes, it is. The BC courts could take that approach because they are putting all their material out, and there is not much of a cost barrier. All you need is an Internet account and a computer. I think the BC courts expect lawyers to be on top of all the most recent material. But there is a little notice on their site that the index may not be current! There is no indication of how often they run the site indexer. The case may be there, but you're not going to find it in a site search if they haven't updated the index since it was placed there.

Besides the judicial and legislative sites, where do you go on the Web?

The University of Toronto has a great site [101] that tells you where different periodicals are available electronically, with links to periodicals available on the Web. For American material, I go to FindLaw [6]. It's fairly well-organized. The search language is useable and the site has a lot of fairly high-quality material. AustLII [33] is a wonderful collection of Australian primary legal sources with value-added features, such as links to judicial consideration of cases and statutes. Recent full-text English cases are now available for viewing and downloading — though not for searching — on Casebase [37]. All of these sites are free of charge.

Would you do legal research with any of the generic Web finding tools like AltaVista [61] or Yahoo! [66]?

I would never create a legal research query similar to what I would put into an electronic commercial service, and just pop it into a generic Web-finding tool. This is partly because the search syntax is not as flexible, but mostly because it is impossible to know much about the actual content that is being searched. I can give you an example of an occasion, though, when a generic Web tool did help locate interesting material. I had a student who was researching redevelopment of inner city neighborhoods for a paper, and she identified "gentrification" as an important term. She put it into a general search engine and up came a couple of papers exactly on her subject. Clearly she needed to conduct her research using a variety of other tools as well, but this was a useful starting point for her. This search was particularly effective because it used a single distinctive term. Search syntax didn't matter, and it was unlikely that there would be a high number of irrelevant documents.

Do you use listservs or newsgroups in connection with legal research?

I do, but I've cut down my memberships dramatically. It was overwhelming. It's too bad, because there were occasional pieces of useful information, but it was too much work to get them. I have found it useful, occasionally, to pose questions to listservs. I did it much more when I was at the University than I do in private practice. Everything I am researching now is confidential, so I am reluctant to pose questions unless the inquiry is extremely generic. I belong to the Canadian Association of Law Libraries list [67] and the Legal Research Network lists [68], which are really the only Canadian lists for legal research. I also belong to a U.S.-based list for people who teach legal research.

What stage are we at with Internet legal research?

In our jurisdiction we are fortunate, because we have our statutes, bills and recent case law up on the Internet. Our federal courts and the Supreme Court of Canada have decisions up at their sites. However, there is very little historical depth. You have to work hard to find the help files to learn how to compose queries. The search syntaxes are not as flexible as those used on the commercial services. We are not at the stage where we can cancel our QuickLaw accounts. I can't see that ever happening, because people who run Net sites are not making money, and it takes a lot of money to build a high-quality research tool. Often, promising leads turn out to be pay-per-view sites with little free information.

It is phenomenal how much material is available on the Internet for free. I don't know how long that will continue. I wonder if some of these sites will eventually become subscription sites. In Canada we have the issue of Crown Copyright, which I don't think you have to worry about in the States. The government could decide to charge users for access to its sites containing legislation and case law. For instance, the BC government sites all make it very clear that the BC government claims copyright in all the material on its site and puts restrictions on what you can do with it. The federal government, fortunately, has disclaimed its copyright.

Has anyone doing legal research been called to task for violating Crown Copyright?

Not Crown Copyright, to my knowledge, but legal publishers have been very concerned about the photocopying of case reports by lawyers. There is a lawsuit before the courts in Ontario against the courthouse library there, with respect to photocopying of reporters. There is a real push for the law firms to pay license fees to the publishers.

Do you ever use a case or statute retrieved from a legislative or judicial Web site without checking a print version?

Sometimes there is no print version. Sometimes the case is reported, but I still take the copy from the Web site and refer to it using the print citation, particularly when the report is not readily available. Because the cases come from sites operated by the courts, I consider them to be reliable. The British Columbia courts have passed a practice directive permitting parties to bring copies of the decisions from the Internet site to court. If the decisions are reported, you have to use the reported citation to refer to them. However, you can submit the version from the Internet to the court. For statutes, where every word counts, I would always check the electronic version against the print version. On occasion, I have found errors in the electronic version.

In the States, at least at the trial court level, there is a growing acceptance of citing cases by a Lexis or Westlaw form of citation. Some states, such as Montana, encourage what they call a "medium-neutral" electronic citation to be added to the other citations. The Montana form also will standardize internal paragraph references. Is anything like that going on in Canada?

We do not have any recognized form of vendor-neutral citation. Each court adopts its own rules about citation. However, most of the courts accept the rules in the *Canadian Guide to Uniform Legal Citation* put out by McGill University. The fourth edition deals quite extensively with citing electronic documents. It requires that you give the print citation first and then give an alternate citation for the electronic version. In some ways, we in Canada are a little further along in standardized internal references, because QuickLaw never used star pagination. Instead, QuickLaw and several Canadian legal publishers started using paragraph numbering. Some Canadian courts even release their decisions with the paragraphs already numbered. Some publishers have recently chosen to go with star pagination instead, but most cases are now published with paragraph numbering. In my view, paragraph numbering is preferable because, no matter what version of the case anyone has, you can have standardized internal references.

How do you save documents from the Internet?

All the material from our BC court site is in ASCII text. The Supreme Court of Canada documents are beautifully formatted. We have the choice of getting them in rich text format (RTF), as a WordPerfect document, in hypertext markup language (HTML), or in plain ASCII text. More and more sites are putting a lot of effort into formatting and are providing options for taking documents off in a word-processing format.

Which format do you usually take?

It depends on what I want to do with the document. Sometimes I'm just printing it out and I'm not going to keep an electronic copy. For that, the HTML usually looks quite nice, and I'll just print it out. If it is something I want to save, and might want to use sections of in another document, I'll take it off in a word-processing format. Our office uses Word, so I would use something compatible with Word, like RTF. I have saved things in HTML and then blocked parts of them to use as internal quotations in documents.

If you were going to submit an electronic version of a case with court papers, how would you handle it?

The Supreme Court of Canada decisions come out beautifully just printed from the browser. The downloaded decisions are in one language only. Because we're a dual-language country, often the court likes to see the decisions in English and French. It might have a slightly different meaning, and may raise a whole new area for consideration. If I am taking a Supreme Court of Canada decision to court, I would copy it from the *Supreme Court Reports*, which is the official reporter for the court and publishes the decisions in English and French. The BC decisions are on the Internet in ASCII text. They don't look as nice, but that's how the court has chosen to put them up. I feel it's better not to fiddle with them, but to give them to the court the way they are on the site. Once again, if the decision has been reported and I have ready access to the print version, I would submit the print version to the court.

Do you have an extensive set of bookmarks for legal research?

Most of my legal bookmarks [92] are on the bookmark list on my Web site. Our librarian has an enormous list of bookmarks. She is putting together a database of links, and is quite disciplined about capturing them. I've been content to let her take on the major task of being the keeper of Web sites for the firm, but I do bookmark links when I find one that I think is going to be useful again. Because most of my research is restricted to legal issues, there are a limited number of sites that are useful to me.

What can a lawyer who brings you a research request do to help you do the best job?

They can make sure I know as many of the facts as are relevant to the question. Otherwise, I end up having to make assumptions, and I might not make the right ones. I might over-research, because I would have to research the problem based on various factual assumptions. It's important for the lawyer to have a realistic understanding of the work involved. Some questions are very narrow and can be answered quickly. Some are quite difficult and may move along on several different tracks. It's important to have an appreciation of what's involved in researching the law of three or four different jurisdictions. As Canadian lawyers, we look outside our own jurisdiction, and outside our own country, much more than American researchers do. In a given research project, I might be looking at the laws of Australia, England and the United States, as well as all the Canadian jurisdictions.

Do you have a favorite Internet search story you'd like to tell?

The Internet contains information not readily available from conventional sources. While looking for material dealing with fair use and libraries in the copyright context, I found a site where someone had mounted all the intervenor briefs from U.S. litigation on the subject. This material was very useful because it summarized the law and dealt extensively with the policy issues involved. When I first started teaching legal research, I discovered a site with syllabi for advanced legal research courses. It helped me a lot to get access to this type of information. That is what's so intriguing about the Internet — all these unconnected bits of information that individuals have made available because they think they're important and may be of use to someone. Unfortunately, the Internet is becoming so clogged and full of garbage that it's harder to get to those nuggets now.

What do you mean, "clogged and full of garbage"?

When you run a search using the general search engines, you often end up with a hit list comprised of personal hobby pages, X-rated sites, and things that don't seem to be even tangentially related to your search terms. You have to wade through a lot to get to the highly relevant material. It takes a while for the pages to load, with all the advertising and all the graphics. The entries at the top of the hit lists are sometimes there because the site owner has paid the search engine for a priority listing, not because the site is highly relevant. Often, internal pages on sites are not indexed, meaning that your search cannot retrieve those pages. When I decide how I am going to do something, time is money. I find that the time it takes to do an Internet search usually outweighs the value of the information obtained, compared with other sources. For this reason, I rarely use the general search engines for any form of legal research. I prefer a good list of legal bookmarks that enables me to go directly to a highly relevant site.

What attracts you to online research?

One of the beauties of online research is the ability to do random access searching, to be freed from the confines of indexing, to be able to interact directly with the text. It's fun to pose a sophisticated Boolean query that goes through all that text and brings up highly relevant documents. Certain talents are needed to do this well. Part of it is knowing which databases are available. Part of it is having a good understanding of the legal problem you are addressing. Part of it is science. Part of it is art. Having a flexible mind helps, because it is crucial to think of all the ways that the author of the document might have expressed the concept. Marrying that with a detailed understanding of the search syntax, and being able to manipulate that syntax confidently, is essential. Most people are not familiar enough with the search syntax to manipulate it effectively, and become quite frustrated with electronic searching. Because of the challenges of full-text searching, more and more people have turned to things like hierarchical tables of contents, digests, and Key Numbers, which use standardized language and permit you to research in a manner more like print research. These tools provide another useful way to approach electronic research, but they remove the researcher's contact with the full text.

That's part of the reason I like to augment my Boolean research with natural language searching. For a lot of searchers, natural language searching gets them back in touch with using full text, and enables them to pull material up that they might not find when using traditional print or Boolean research methods. With my students, even if I could get them to understand the search syntax, often they just didn't think flexibly enough about the search terms: What are all the different ways somebody could say this, and how many different forms could those words take? Although natural language search engines help by searching on truncated forms of the words, most do not address the problem of synonyms and alternate search terms. Most online research is still very literal. If the query is one word or even one character off, the document will not be retrieved. That's all it takes.

If a legal research student doesn't get anything else from you, what do you want them to get?

The first thing would be to think carefully about their problem before they start, to ensure that they aren't taking too narrow an approach, and to ensure that they understand the question asked. Second, as they conduct their research, they should re-define, rethink, and re-frame their issues continuously, so as not to be limited by their initial characterization of the problem. Third, I would tell them to start writing early, not to feel that they have to do all their research before they start writing. Writing forces the analysis, enhances the analysis, gets you to ask questions earlier, and to think a little harder about where you are going and what you still need to do. They don't have to be beautifully shaped sentences. For most of the things I write now, I start with the outliner that's built into Word. I prepare a bare outline of issues, and flesh that out as I identify the sub-issues. I add the case names relevant to each issue and take it from there, one layer at a time. It really helps to get a framework. It helps to keep me focused. It disciplines me to have my issues broken down into sub-issues. Because most of us are now writing electronically, often we can get lost in a document. The outline can be collapsed and expanded. I can work on just a little section of it at a time and I can move things around easily.

Super Searcher Secrets

- *On documenting the search...*Every time I open a book, I write down the name, author, year and usually the publisher. For loose-leaf books, I always write down the date of the most recent release I've checked. When I look in digests, I write down the headings I've looked under. When I do computer searches, I write down my search string, the databases I went into and the date.

- *On organizing the strategy...*I keep a fairly structured file while I'm working on anything. I always have a brown accordion folder with inside sub-folders and I'll have a different one for each issue. For some projects I might have six or seven issues. I've watched people struggle with being able to write once they've done the research. They may be able to get through the research okay, but then they have a pile of stuff they can't deal with for writing. If you can organize your research papers, it helps that process.

► *On planning before logging on...*I do a fair amount. I always make a list of keywords, synonyms and alternate words, and think about which words should be truncated. I think about what databases to search and make a note of them. Then, as I do the search, I refine it and check off what I've searched. Depending on how complex the search is, and how many alternate terms it includes, my search plan is more like a diagram, with several columns of alternate terms separated by the appropriate connectors.

► *On initial file and field selection...*My first step usually is to search digests if I can, rather than going straight to full text. I search on small summaries of the cases in files that have fairly comprehensive coverage. For searching in the States, I tend to go to Westlaw first and search in the synopsis and digest fields, rather than the full text of the database. To test those results, I might search again using natural language in full text, and compare the search results.

► *On building a search...*In online research, I definitely start narrow, looking for something that's very particular, very much on my subject. In hardcopy research, I often start the other way around, by looking at textbooks. On most projects, I work from both ends, starting more broadly in textbooks to get a conceptual context and references to leading cases, and searching narrowly online, looking for cases that are specifically on my fact pattern.

► *On aiding analysis...*I would tell them to start writing early, not to feel that they have to do all their research before they start writing. Writing forces the analysis, enhances the analysis, gets you to ask questions earlier and to think a little harder about where you are going and what you still need to do. They don't have to be beautifully shaped sentences. For most of the things I write now, I start with the outliner that's built into Word. I prepare a bare outline of issues and flesh that out as I identify the sub-issues.

George R. Jackson

Think Bibliographically

George R. Jackson, J.D., M.L.S., is a reference librarian and professor of legal research and advanced legal research at the University of Minnesota School of Law. Mr. Jackson is an expert in government documents and integrated legal research methodology.

g-jack@tc.umn.edu
www.tc.umn.edu/nlhome/m212/g-jack/

How did you get into legal research?

I went to law school and probably should not have been there. I didn't know what I was doing there. Practicing law wasn't really what I wanted to do. I wasn't adequately trained for research in law school. That added to my uncertainty about practicing law. I made research my focus, found my way over to librarianship, and got my library science degree. That way I could stay involved in law without litigating or practicing law. Now it's a joy being able to share a useful skill with other people.

Describe the setting of your reference work.

I'm one of four librarians. We take reference requests over the phone and in person, from students, faculty, the Bar and *pro se* [Latin: for himself, i.e., not represented by an attorney] patrons. We have levels of priority. Our highest level of clientele is our faculty. They give us our most complicated questions. There is a tremendous influx of students at certain times of the year when there is a writing assignment, a cite-checking assignment or a law review being issued. Aside from those times, about one-third to forty percent of our requests come from faculty, another thirty to forty percent from our student body, and the remainder from the Bar and *pro se* patrons.

What sorts of things do faculty ask for?

Frequently they have a citation and want us to retrieve the document. Frequently they want a bibliography of articles and books on a given topic. They may want us to find cases that would help their research or that make a certain point. It can be almost anything. The form in which they want it varies widely. Some want just a bibliography. Others want a bibliography with the original hardcopy sources, not photocopies. Some want photocopies of documents and others want electronic printouts.

How quickly do you turn a project around?

With the faculty, generally immediately, except when they ask us to watch developments on a certain topic and update them periodically. If it is a big project where they want a complete bibliography, you have to buy a little time. Hopefully, they will have a couple of weeks. For a lot of things, it's last-minute business just like everyone else. People stand at the reference desk and wait. When it gets really busy, we call it triage. You can have six people standing in the office when a faculty member calls. You have to take care of faculty requests first, so you give everybody else a little something to go on, and get back to them in depth later, after you clear the faculty request.

Do you have an intake procedure for new reference requests?

Whichever one of us is on the reference desk conducts a reference interview. I always ask what they think they are looking for. If they have a reference, I like to find out where they found it. I try to get a couple of different access points of bibliographic information. You do try to make sure that what they are asking for is what they want. It involves helping them identify what they really need. People have a lot of misunderstandings about law and legal terminology. Frequently I give a mini legal research tutorial or a five-minute sketch on what kinds of authority there are. The law isn't necessarily just a rule written in a book. The law is organic, and that is unsettling to people. I'm not acting as an authority. I explain the bibliographic information, how to get at it, and how the sources of information relate to each other, without offering an opinion on it. If I don't know the substantive legal area, I ask them to educate me a little bit. You get as much hard information from them as you can, and then develop the strategy.

Do you document reference requests when they come in?

In other places where I have worked I have done that. Every time I took one in, I wrote down the person's identification, the request and whatever information they had. If it was going to be a long project, I kept a list of things I checked. Requests repeat themselves. Faculty often call back and ask a related question six months later. Those files can be very useful.

Law schools teach beginning law students stock approaches to legal research. When you teach advanced legal research, do you go further into those approaches, or does the approach itself change?

For the most part, it goes out the window. Those strategies are in the legal research books. I allude to them and we talk about them a little bit in class. There is no universal application of them. In my advanced legal research courses, the students are doing what amounts to an independent study. Some of them are concentrating in administrative law. Others are totally in common law. They pick their own topics. There is not a single model I can overlay on everybody. When you get into advanced legal research you have to analyze what the authority is, and then go at it bibliographically. You have to figure out what you need and where it is going to be. Who's responsible for that information?

Do you have checklists or pathfinders for some kinds of research problems?

In the reference office we have many. We have approaches to finding case law, different kinds of primary material, secondary sources and periodical literature. We have some topical ones, such as tax and securities law. We have certain jurisdictional ones, such as for Canadian or British legal research. I'm putting some samples of pathfinders that were produced in my class on my Web site. It takes so darn long that I've only got four of them up.

Does a patron sometimes say "get me everything on" a certain topic?

Among the categories of patrons, there are different levels of research we'll do. For faculty, we'll do anything. They will ask for everything out there. They sometimes ask more than one of us to do it, and play us off against each other. They are hedging their bets that one will get something the other won't. If the patron is an attorney or an alum, I might make suggestions to help narrow and target the request.

When a faculty member says "get me everything on," are you able to follow up and see if they really needed that?

They usually are shot-gunning their requests. People who ask that type of question are the least likely to facilitate that type of follow-up. They generally are people who don't want to spend much time in their reference interview analyzing what they need and then mapping out the strategy. They are using a scatter-shot approach. I don't think most of them want a lot of follow-up. If you do give them a fairly complete bibliography or list of case citations, analyzing the list and figuring out what that universe of information is all about often helps them begin to narrow it on their own. So I don't think their approach is totally invalid, but it's a little frustrating when you think, "Boy, I bet I could pare this down." On the other hand, I often like coming in on things from a global or mega-approach. I know the bibliographic tools to do it.

Do you run a project straight through and then deliver the final package, or do you use an iterative approach where you check back with the patron at various stages along the way?

That depends on the project. Often I call people back. I usually try to get as much information as I can up front. But it is related to what we said about there not being one single approach to legal research. The research process itself may be iterative, and that will impact on the contacts with the patron. Research is cyclical, and it's not always the same cycle. As you do one thing, you learn a little bit more, and that will alter your strategy. Often I go back to the patron—whether it's a law firm librarian, one of our faculty members or an attorney downtown—and ask them more questions, saying, "I found this. Is this right or wrong? Am I getting warm or cold?"

Do you keep records of where and how you searched?

Even though I teach my students that that's a really good thing to do, I don't do it. In jobs where I used forms and documented things, I definitely appreciated it. I documented the strategy, the terminology, the combination of search terms, the fields and the descriptors or subject headings I used. Here, I often wish I'd done that. Patrons frequently come back and say, "I'd like you to branch off here and go this way with it." You *do* save yourself work when you document your research as you go along.

What is your preferred method for checking whether a case is still good law?

An electronic citator on Lexis [54, see Appendix A] or Westlaw [60]. I don't use hardbound citators. Shepard's keeps subdividing its publications. There are more and more things to pay for and we are subscribing to fewer and fewer. We do have Shepard's for Minnesota and Shepard's Northwestern, but we wouldn't buy all the other regional Shepards. That is one thing that is clearly more user-friendly and usable online. In hardbound, with all the supplements, you go through a supplement-gathering process and still wonder what you might have missed. Also, in a place like this, those materials frequently wander off.

What's your preferred method for finding cases that construe a statute or an administrative regulation?

I start in an annotated code for browsability. Eye contact is important. You will get cross-references and some references to secondary material. I frequently also will Shepardize or KeyCite. Depending on how elusive it is, I often use the statutory cite as a search term. The online services are getting better with their equivalencies, but I don't think they're there yet, so I use pieces of the citation in proximity. You leave out the abbreviation and focus on the numbers. You might get some false hits, but you're not as likely to miss something.

How much planning do you do before logging on for an electronic research session?

Usually none, except for locating the database I need. Does the file exist on the system? If it's primary material, that's all I'm looking for. If it's secondary source material like law reviews or treatises, I'm more likely to go into GUIDE on Lexis, or SCOPE or IDEN on Westlaw, to see exactly what they contain. Depending on the type of material, I may go a little deeper to see if what I want will be there. With law reviews online, some files contain every article and other files select articles only. I've had to call customer service sometimes, because I was uncertain that I had determined correctly whether what I wanted was there.

How do you feel about starting research online as opposed to beginning with preparatory research offline?

A colleague and I were teaching a legal research class, and she would say, "You should never go online first thing. That's not the proper place to start any research." I said, "It's not too bad to do with patrons who ask for everything on x, y or z." The scatter-shot approach can work. You get online for five minutes, toss out some words, see one or two relevant hits, look them over, get some new vocabulary and strategies, and get back on using those. I definitely think that's a valid way to go. Before you ever start, you figure on doing more than one search.

How do you usually build a search?

The more I already know about the topic or the database, the more narrowly I begin. The less I know, or the less certain I am, the more broadly I begin. I was trained first on Lexis, back when you got hit with a search charge when you hit the TRANSMIT key, but not when you modified a search. That encouraged searchers to start more broadly than they otherwise might have. Out of habit, I still start somewhat broad and narrow down to one thing that gives me context. Sometimes you have a solid access point like a party name, an author or a date. That narrows it down, but the rest of the initial search statement is broad.

What do you do when you are finding too much material?

I either talk to the requestor to see how to narrow it down, or I have them look at what I'm getting to see why I'm getting so much. If I did the reference interview correctly, I shouldn't be getting too much. If I am getting too much, I generally summarize what I'm getting and have another conference to sort out where to go from there. I want to rule out defects in the reference interview before I continue struggling with the search.

How about the opposite problem, when you aren't finding anything?

The requestor definitely wants an answer and I'll wonder, "Well, maybe there isn't anything." Often we are researching points of first impression. It's very unsettling to people. When I report that there is no case authority on the issue, they don't accept it, until I explain why. How many trial court decisions don't get published? It's not that this has never happened in our jurisdiction. It's just that there is no published decision on it and, therefore, no legal authority that we can find. Finding nothing might prompt me to jump into secondary material for an explanation for why I am coming up with that black hole. Secondary material might talk about gaps and open questions.

How often are you searching full text?

About sixty percent of the time.

How do you approach full-text searching compared with searching an index or a bibliographic database?

It depends on what you have to go in with. If I have a phrase, searching for it is a good way to narrow the search. I can use more proximity connectors. If things are really bad, I might try using a cluster of parentheses with general terms, something you would never do in an index or bibliographic database.

How long was the longest search statement you remember ever using?

Two lines would be a really long search statement. When I was younger and less experienced, I would put in a much more complicated search statement. Now I generally get everything onto one line. Instead of using overly sophisticated search statements, you can start by narrowing the universe of information by the file you select. Learn to use more restrictors, whether date, citation, type of publication or author. The combination of file selection, restrictors, proximity and phrases is very narrowing. I usually try to do something like that; it amazes me when other people don't.

During the search, how do you decide if you are getting the right stuff?

On Westlaw I display hits in term mode and on Lexis in KWIC (Key Word In Context) or VAR KWIC (Variable Key Word In Context). KWIC usually provides enough context. If it's not evident on its face, I use the tools that the electronic medium offers. I do a Term Locate, a FOCUS or, in a Web browser, a Find on Page. I look at the terms of my search statement in the context of the document.

When do you gravitate more toward Westlaw, and when toward Lexis?

The longer I use both of them, the more interchangeable they become. It might depend on which service has the database I want. If I'm looking for foreign and international materials, Lexis has more. If I'm looking for cases and I want to use West Topic and Key Numbers, there is nothing like Westlaw. On Lexis, when you find one case on point, you can find more like it with the command More Like This.

What do you think of the Web versions of Westlaw and Lexis?

I've only used them a couple of times, and I hated them. Each time they revise those systems, they dumb them down. They are making them simpler to use on their face, but they are taking away features that allow me to do more tightly controlled searches. On Lexis I enjoyed being able to stack my commands. You go in, select your sources, do your search, choose your display format, and output. You could get in and out without having to wait for each library, file and search screen to load. You're not able to combine fields in a complex search as easily as you could with the old keystroke commands. It seems to me that you are encouraged to do simple, more limited types of searching. My reservation is that it gives people a false sense of security. I see a lot of students who think they have done a pretty good search of x, y or z, and it will turn out that their search has been in an inappropriate database to begin with, as well as totally inadequate or inappropriate.

What factors lead you to use the Internet for a particular project?

The type of patron: What tools can I use for them? Our subscription agreements don't allow us to use some of our services for all patrons. That might necessitate using the Internet. I look right away at the date of the materials. If I need material from much before 1990, the Internet probably is not going to be my first place to go. Another big factor is whether I need primary or secondary material. There are a lot of reliable sites with primary authority, like GPO Access [12]. Their search features are getting better. They are adding content all the time. The Internet is weak in secondary authority.

You and Linda Swanson have prepared a set of documents on "Internet Strategies for the Paralegal in Minnesota" [95]. The first page is an outline and its major headings are hyperlinked to the more detailed pages. I like that arrangement. You get an initial, comprehensible overview so you can keep your sense of place.

During the advanced legal research class last semester, we started perfecting the pathfinders that I have put on my Web site. Most of that came from my students' comments. When you are doing research, do you want to read the whole thing or do you want to be able to get to the page that talks about the stuff you need? They were very critical of documents that were hard to negotiate, headings that didn't say what they were about and not being able to zero in on information. We need to think about searcher behavior. You might be looking at a very good page, but if you have to scroll or search through more than a dozen screens full of information, never sure that, if you scroll the rest of the way, you'll come to what you want, you might decide to go to your next AltaVista hit without bothering to find out. I do that all the time. If something doesn't go quickly enough, I hit Stop, go back, and hit the next one on the list.

Are there times when you would start your research on the Internet?

Seldom. I'm not in a mind-set yet where I would begin on the Internet very often. If it was a certain patron and it was primary material, perhaps. Some publications, though, even a few law reviews, appear only on the Internet, with no hardcopy equivalent. The Internet is the only place where some foreign materials appear.

Where do you go when you do go on the Internet?

You try to evaluate the authority of sites: Who put the site there? There are some very good sites, like GPO Access and Thomas [15], where the authority is clear. Many state-sponsored sites look reliable to me; I trust their authority over some other sites. It helps with authority if you find out about a site in library literature, a government document, a newsletter or a listserv for law librarians. If it's not a governmental source of authority, the next level down is law schools. WashLaw [29] and Villanova [23] have great sites. Pitt has a nice site called JURIST [26] with a lot of information. Cornell's Legal Information Institute 9 (LII) [27] has been around for a long time.

Your primary issue is authority. Are other factors like searchability a close second, or are they vastly secondary?

Vastly. The site *must* have authority or I don't consider it. A lot of our research is the basis for somebody's writing. For myself, I might do more adventurous searching to arrive at the authority. On the way I might look at some less authoritative sites, or ones I'm not sure of, because they are more searchable. I might go into FindLaw [6] and do a search there.

Suppose you're looking for something and don't know yet where it's going to be. Once you find it, you are going to look at its authority, but at the finding stage, where might you go?

After using my known sources and not finding what I need, I might go through the typical approaches like search engines and hierarchical subject directories. But I am still looking for authority. If I go to AltaVista [61], I plug in a search string that I think should appear because of the subject, along with a term representing the authority, such as "State of Montana" or "Governor's Office." It's almost like what we were talking about earlier on Westlaw or Lexis: doing a citation search with a keyword or phrase when you have one hard bit of information. You know the author or you know the date, but you don't know anything else about the topic. You put in a search string like "search and seizure" and the name of the state. I do a couple of searches like that in different search engines or catalogs like AltaVista, Excite [63], Yahoo! [66] and a legal one like FindLaw. I might search the archives of a good discussion group for a pointer to the source. I look at *The Virtual Chase* [3] and *Law Library Resource Xchange* (LLRX) [1] for articles that will point me to the source. I use a combination of tools, because they all have such limited coverage of the Web. If I don't find it that way, I might think, "Who's the authority for this?" and "Who has an interest in this?" I'll look to see if an authority like the American Bar Association [31] or the American Law Institute [91] has some material, and I'll see if they have any publications or links to other sites.

Sometimes you are not really looking for the document on the Web. You are looking for the site. Once at the site, you look for the document.

Exactly. I do that a lot.

Have you ever had a search where you felt sure something should be on the Internet but you were never able to find it?

Oh, yes. Lots of times. Sometimes it could mean the information really is not there, but other times it could be there and just not indexed in the finding tools. If I'm frustrated enough, I'll ask some colleagues, "Have you had experience with this?" I might ask the reference librarians on the listservs. I've gone so far as to do a search in newspapers on Lexis or Westlaw to see if there are any articles that mention electronic publications or Web sites on the subject. Sometimes I'll call an organization or a government entity and say, "I know this publication has to be available somewhere on the Web and I'm just not finding it." I used to have this problem with some of the AIDS surveillance reports from the Centers for Disease Control. I actually called the authority or somebody interested in that field to see if they had anything.

Which listservs do you use?

I use LAW-LIB [70]. I use one for reference librarians, LAWLIB-REF-L [71], where they talk about research strategy or types of materials for particular research. I use GOVDOC-L [69] because I am a government documents librarian. That's an excellent source because government documents librarians are very thorough. They are extremely critical of the government and they have had a great impact on government electronic publishing. Their discussions are often very detailed. They will talk about what is there, what isn't, how much of it is, how useful it is, and whether it meets the statutory criteria for making government information available to people. If you use a lot of listservs, as I used to — and I actually used to read them all — you could spend your whole day. I'd have all listservs filtered into different files in my email, and during the week I'd spend several hours going through and clearing it out. Usually I am looking for discussion of sources, how to use sources or how to do research. There is a lot of other discussion that's not as useable, but those three lists do include that kind of discussion.

Suppose you are talking to a skilled Westlaw or Lexis searcher who is now going to launch into Internet legal research. What are you going to tell them?

Lots of caveats about date restriction, the authority and reliability of sites and the lack of standardization. Let's say you are searching for attorney general opinions across seventeen states. They may be on the Internet, but there is no uniformity in format, searchability or even the software used to put up the databases. There is no global uniformity across jurisdiction and types of information like there is in Lexis and Westlaw. You have to be prepared to roll with the punches, follow the menu and be a little disappointed. It is going to take more work, more time, and your final outcome may less comprehensive.

If they're going into a concrete, defined area for a definitive purpose, then I'd be more encouraging. I'd tell them about the differences between search engines and directories, about how they gather information from the Web, about the small percentage of the Web they cover, about their indexes lagging behind the actual content of the Web, and about some of the reasons Web search tools hit on all kinds of irrelevant documents. Then I'd show them a few features of Web browsers. I'd show them how to find text in the page, how to print, how to download, how to save a file, and how to email yourself a copy of a page.

Are you still bookmarking a lot of sites for fear you might not be able to find them again?

I still bookmark sites but I use the bookmarks less. I'm able to remember the first part of the uniform resource locator (URL) string for most of the best legal sites. Often I'll remember a good compilation of links in an article on LLRX. I'll go to LLRX and find the list rather than wrestle with my bookmarks. The search engines and directories have improved significantly during the last couple of years. A bookmark for a URL that I cannot remember or find someplace like LLRX might be out of date anyway, so I'll search for it again using a search engine or directory.

Do you have a favorite Internet search story?

I had a student from the law review looking for a newspaper article. I probably should have started with the Internet, but I tried everything else first. I looked in hardcopy bibliographic sources, our library catalog and bibliographic utilities as well. Then I tried Lexis and Westlaw. Then I tried periodical directories like Ulrich's [100]. I did all those things and just wasn't getting it. It turns out that the newspaper is published only on the Internet.

Why are you a searcher? What do you like about it?

One reason is that it's logical. You are using language, you are using logic and you are constantly evaluating what you do as you go along. It's an argument I can have with myself: I can ask myself questions as I go along and develop the search. Another reason is that you learn as you go along; you develop skills. Another part of it is like the satisfaction of cleaning your kitchen: It's so nice when you find the answer. You get visible results. Another part of it is that you get to be a generalist; you don't have to specialize in much of anything. We do have a foreign law specialist, and I might have more facility with certain documents or questions than some of our other librarians. But basically you are a generalist, and you deal with a lot of different subjects. You don't need to have a terribly long attention span, because right now you might be helping someone find child support payment guidelines, and an hour later you might have a human rights issue in Nepal.

What general warnings do you give your students?

The most important thing is to be really sure what they've got when they find something. With electronic sources, when something pops up on your screen, it's easy to feel a sense of accomplishment or reward and think, "Oh, I got what I need." You might have gotten something, but you need to be sure what you've searched, and hence what you've gotten. You need to be sure you've searched everything you thought you searched. You have to observe the scope of the database. You need to know whether it's really full text or selected full text. You need to know the date range of a file's coverage. You need to know which source documents are included in the file. I see students do a lot of searches in the wrong database. They think they have included tax advice memoranda that were really in a different file. I see them not go back far enough in time.

Super Searcher Secrets

- *On stock legal research strategies taught in law schools...*For the most part, it goes out the window. When you get into advanced legal research, you have to analyze what the authority is and then go at it bibliographically. You have to figure out what you need and where it is going to be. Who's responsible for that information?
- *On alternative ways to find cases construing a statute...* Depending on how elusive it is, I frequently use the statutory cite as a search term. The online services are getting better with their equivalencies, but I don't think they're there yet, so I use pieces of the citation in proximity. You leave out the abbreviation and focus on the numbers.
- *On targeting searches...*Start by narrowing the universe of information by the file you select. Learn to use more restrictors, whether date, citation, type of publication or author. The combination of file selection, restrictors, proximity and phrases is very narrowing.

- *On the dumbing down of online services...*Each time they revise those systems, they dumb them down. They are making them simpler to use on their face, but they are taking away features that allow me to do more tightly controlled searches. It seems to me that you are encouraged to do simple, more limited types of searching. My reservation is that it gives people a false sense of security.

- *On finding authoritative sites...*I am still looking for authority. If I go to AltaVista, I plug in a search string that I think should appear because of the subject, along with a term representing the authority, such as "State of Montana" or "Governor's Office." I look at *The Virtual Chase* and *Law Library Resource Xchange* (LLRX) for articles that will point me to the source. If I don't find it that way, I might think, "Who's the authority for this?" and then, "Who has an interest in this?"

- *On the importance of database selection...*The most important thing is to really be sure what they've got when they find something. You may have gotten something, but you need to be sure what you've searched, and hence what you've gotten. You have to observe the scope of the database. I see students do a lot of searches in the wrong database.

Diana Botluk

Music of the Search

Diana Botluk is reference librarian at The Judge Kathryn J. DuFour Law Library, Columbus School of Law, Catholic University of America in Washington, D.C., and author of *The Legal List*. Diana is involved in the development and presentation of online legal research lectures and workshops for both students and professionals. As a columnist for the *Internet Law Researcher* newsletter, she writes about finding information on the World Wide Web. She co-chairs the Internet Focus Group of the Law Librarians' Society of Washington, D.C., and is an adjunct assistant professor at the University of Maryland, where she teaches both traditional legal research and Online Legal Resources, a course she created.

botluk@law.cua.edu
http://www.lcp.com/The-Legal-List/index.html

How did you get into legal research?

I got into legal research when I was a law student here at Catholic University many years ago. We were going through a great big change. We were just getting Lexis [54, see Appendix A] and Westlaw [60]. I was a student desk attendant at the library. I had always known how to run computers and search them. I'm not a techie; I don't know how to tinker with them or fix them, but I do know how to use them to my benefit. So, I jumped right in, helping other people in the school learn Lexis and Westlaw. That's when I started getting into legal research. If it had been all book-oriented research, I would not have gotten into it quite as much, because I like the online stuff the best. I don't struggle with the hardbound library, but I don't think it would have been my "thing." I've worked here since I graduated.

Tell me a little bit about this exciting new building we're in.

It is lovely. It's a pleasure to come to work here. When we were making plans for this beautiful new building, we had a very forward-thinking committee in terms of electronic connectivity. The library and classrooms are all wired. You can plug in and get online all over the place.

How do patrons come to you? Do they all walk up to the desk? Can they email a request, fax or call you on the phone?

All of the above. The students are mostly walk-ins. The faculty usually emails or calls on the phone. Very rarely is anything faxed, but of course we would accept that, too. We do get a few questions from outsiders. They are not our main focus because it is a private library, but we do try to help them as much as we can.

What realms of legal research do you do?

It could be any kind of law, or research outside of law or something tangential. Each of us has some strengths. My colleague is stronger in D.C. law, for example.

How quickly do you usually have to turn requests around?

Everything varies. We answer on-the-fly questions right away. We can take our time with more in-depth research projects, sometimes up to a couple of weeks. A lot of people think far enough ahead that we get some time. Occasionally we hear, "I'm giving a speech tomorrow and I need this right away. Can you go out and find articles on such-and-such a topic?" If the request is from a student, we're not necessarily going to answer the question for them. We will teach them how to find the answer themselves.

We get questions like "How do I find my regulation in the *Code of Federal Regulations* and how do I update it?" Instead of finding the regulation for them, we show them the index, show them the list of sections and show them how to do it themselves. In that sense, we are part of the teaching process.

Do you conduct a formal reference interview?

We don't do it formally. Usually I'll get an email or voice mail telling me generally why they are looking for the information. Occasionally they will give the wrong information, the wrong date, the wrong spelling of the name or something like that, but I tend to be able to guess what they want anyway. Faculty members are very good about giving us enough information. Students often don't even know what to ask, and we have to guide them.

What kind of product do you usually deliver?

It depends on how big it is. If it is just one article, one case, or something small, we might answer by email, with cut-and-paste text or attachments. If it entails a great number of articles or a lot of written product, or if it's a conglomeration, we print it. They tend to want it printed. They would print it out anyway.

Do you have any formal intake procedure for new research requests?

We don't really have a formal intake procedure. Often our patrons send a group email message to all the reference librarians at once. Whether they know it or not, that tends to be the way for one of us to grab it the fastest. We have to make sure we're not all doing the same project. The one who grabbed it logs it into a calendar program. We can look at the calendar and see if somebody else is working on it. That's as formal as we get.

Has the Internet affected the way you take in or begin on a project?

Yes. If people are looking for something published by an organization or a federal agency — something that I think might be out there on the Web — I will go there first to look for it.

Law schools present stock strategies or approaches to performing legal research. What's your impression of those?

As a teacher, I know you have to teach strategy. Generally you're talking about starting with secondary authority, getting a handle on everything and then on to primary authority. If they don't know anything about the topic, that generally would be a good approach. Obviously you have to evaluate what you are looking for, and then try to take the most efficient route. We start out teaching about treatises and encyclopedias because they have already read books and have already looked at encyclopedias, so this is just putting a legal focus on it. We try to ease them in with something they are already familiar with.

How often do you, in fulfilling a reference question, find yourself using the approach you just described?

I can make a beeline for a source. Sometimes I need some background information. If I grab a Nutshell off the reserve shelf and open it up, it is going to tell me exactly which statutes and which cases are the most important. I don't have to start with the index to the code or anything like that.

What is an example of a more in-depth project that may take a couple of weeks?

Since the research we are doing is for faculty members, it tends to go more into writing articles or giving speeches than into preparing cases. Frequently they want fifty-state surveys on some kind of legislation or court rule. Which courts have this particular rule and how is it different?

Are you sometimes asked to "get me everything on" a certain topic?

They don't put it in quite those terms. They want a literature survey on such-and-such a topic. I take that to mean that I am going to search for books and articles in the appropriate index, find what I can and get back to them.

Do you run a project straight through without communicating again with the patron, or is it more iterative, where you check back to see if you're getting the right stuff?

I usually try to produce something they can look at first, unless I completely do not understand the question. Then, obviously, I'll call them back and ask them to give me a bit more. Usually I'll try to produce something that attempts to answer the question, and say, "If you need to go in a different direction, will you get back to me and we can pursue that?"

Do you keep records of where and how you researched?

We have the calendar where we log in the projects. Each one is annotated to let other people—as well as yourself—know where you stand on it and how much further it needs to go. If we complete it right away, we don't include as much detail. But if we work on it a little there and a little here, it will be detailed. We don't do it so much for the sake of documenting the project as we do to make staff collaboration smoother.

In your setting, does budget affect your research very often?

It affects me a great deal in that I don't have to worry about budget at all. I have unlimited Lexis and Westlaw. Since we pay a flat rate, I don't have to worry about whether I can get on and tinker, or do the most precise search, and I don't have to worry about getting it cheaper somewhere else. We have never had to think about hitting the TRANSMIT key. It has always been a flat rate based on so much per student or per password, with unlimited access and unlimited searching.

How is your research time divided between hardcopy library and electronic sources?

For the research projects, I'd say it's ninety-five percent electronic. The hardcopy is used more in teaching the students how to do research. For most of the first year, with the incoming students, it's mostly hardcopy. As they move up, we teach them more online.

What factors contribute to so much of your work being electronic?

When a faculty member wants an in-depth research project done, they also use their own research assistants. If they want all the cases on a particular topic, they send the research assistant out to do that, because they know how to do it. They save the more outside or tangential questions, and the ones they don't think the research assistants are able to handle as efficiently, for us. Those tend to be questions for which we might not have the resources on the shelf, or something, like a fifty-state survey, for which we do have the resources, but that is much more easily done online.

Is there a particular hardcopy resource you especially like or use often, for which there is no good online substitute as yet?

I'm thinking more in terms of what I can find online but still prefer in hardcopy. That might be something like the *United States Code Annotated*. I prefer to browse through the book rather than search it online. That's true of any kind of code. By its nature, it's arranged by subject matter already. Browsing through pages can key you in to where you want to be. Of course, you can browse through pages online, too, but it's so much quicker to flip the pages with your fingers than press the button and wait for it to come up. Also, it's sometimes valuable to browse through an index and look at the outline that human beings have put together. Keyword searching works for very specific topics. When you have a more general topic, the index approach is a lot easier. You appreciate those human-put-together resources. When you have to search a lot of jurisdictions at once, that's a different story, and you want to approach it with an online source.

How often do you find yourself in the *Decennial Digest*?

Never. I have to teach them, so I do open them occasionally, but I never use them for real research. If I am doing research that I could do in a *Decennial Digest*, I turn to Westlaw because of my unlimited access.

Why are we teaching students to do things in a way we ourselves would never do them?

I think the theory is that they might be going to go to a law firm that doesn't have Lexis or Westlaw. That made sense about ten years ago, but I don't think it does anymore. Almost everybody who practices law provides themselves with at least one or the other of those services. There is another theory that you have to look at, feel and touch the resource in print before you can get online in this cyberspace world and picture it. I don't know that I agree with that one, either.

Are there some other resources in the traditional hardcopy library that you consider more or less obsolete?

The *Index of Legal Periodicals* and the *Legal Resource Index* go back in electronic format to 1980. Any time I am looking for law review articles post-1980, I search the index online, and that makes the hardcopy indexes obsolete. The only time I open those books is if I need something more historical. Shepard's — that's a big one. I never Shepardize with books unless, of course, I am teaching somebody how to do it.

What's your preferred method for checking whether the holding of a case is still good law?

I Shepardize it, but I Shepardize it online. I use multiple tools. I use AutoCite and InstaCite, and now there's KeyCite.

What's your preferred method of finding case law that gives statutory construction where you already have the statute citation?

Annotated code, no question about it. I still start with the books because I find it easier to flip through the pages. You can do that online. If you already have the code section, that's easy. You can pull up the *United States Code Annotated* or *United States Code Service* by section, and the annotation is there. I might have to do it both ways if I need to bring it right up-to-date and the online version is more current than the pocket part.

It sounds to me like you might be what Barbara Quint calls a grasshopper searcher, somebody who hops online without any angst over what you're going to do when you get there.

Yes. I understand the process some people go through in preparation, because we used to use the Dialog [48] databases, and we were paying the same rates law firms were paying. We would sit and prepare the search before we did it. We don't do that much any more. Our flat-rate access has a great deal to do with this. I have the luxury of being able to hop online, try to find something and revise it if it didn't work the first time.

How often do you consult the documentation for an online service prior to logging on?

In hardcopy, never. If I need to check what's in a file or library, I do it online. I go through the GUIDE library on Lexis or the IDEN database on Westlaw. That happens almost every day. I might be looking for a particular source and not know the file name. As far as the how-to of searching is concerned, I almost never look at the documentation.

Typically, how do you build a search?

I usually start narrow and broaden it if I need to. Trying to focus exactly where I want to be is usually my best approach. I would start searching broadly only if I didn't have something narrow to begin with. I might not even try to do keyword searching if it were too broad. I would go a different way. For keyword searching, it's much more efficient if I have a narrow focus.

If you're getting too much material, even though you tried to start narrow, what do you do to focus the search?

It depends on whom it's for. If you're getting too much, you may need to go back to the patron and ask how we might be able to narrow it. A lot of times you narrow it by finding just the most recent items, and then limit by date or by some kind of geographic restriction.

Do you think differently when you're in full text than when you are in a bibliographic file?

If I'm in a bibliographic file, I can more easily just type in some search terms. If I'm in a full-text file, I may want to think about restricting the search to portions of the document, like the headline or the name. With a bibliographic file, the entries are so brief that you can search the whole thing.

Do you consult controlled vocabularies or thesauri?

In a sense I do. I don't actually look it up in a book, but I may do one broad search to figure out what the index terms are. Then I'll do another search using what I found from the first search.

Have you ever looked at published electronic queries designed to, say, update an ALR annotation?

I have seen them, but I can't say that I've ever actually used one. I once constructed a search statement as elaborate as those are. I had a very specific request from a faculty member involving certain rules or code texts in a full-text database. It got so long that I couldn't fit the whole thing in the search query box. I usually wouldn't get that elaborate. For people who are not comfortable with online searching, those published queries are definitely good tools.

During the search, what record format do you look at first to see if you're getting the right stuff?

The KWIC format on Lexis. The way Westlaw presents material now almost makes the term obsolete. You can scroll down and see where the highlights are. I usually use plain KWIC and not VAR KWIC (Variable KWIC). Twenty-five words seem to be enough to see what is going on.

What causes you to gravitate toward either Lexis or Westlaw rather than the other?

It's a combination of things, but content has a lot to do with it. If you want cases, Westlaw has been publishing them in the Key Number System for many decades. They are one up in case law searching, and I always turn there first. An example of the content I like better on Lexis is their federal legislation libraries and files. I turn to them first for that. Then there's the matter of which system you learn first and which you hold in your heart. I did learn Lexis a little bit earlier than Westlaw, so I tend to have more of an emotional grasp on Lexis. That might be the reason I keep turning to them for news articles even though, several years ago, Westlaw put plenty of news articles on its system.

Are there differences in features that will tug you in the direction of one of those services over the other?

I can give you an example of a feature that you probably aren't thinking of. They provide us with stand-alone printers. One of them gives us constant problems, and when we are experiencing problems, instead of spending a half day on the phone with customer service, we jump on the other service.

Are there other online law sources that you use to any great extent?

We do have LegalTrac. It's used more by the students. The same database of material is available on Lexis and Westlaw. We'd probably do it on Lexis and Westlaw from our desktop.

What factors lead you to hop onto the Internet for legal research rather than Lexis or Westlaw?

It depends on content. On the Internet, I would be looking for material that I couldn't find on Lexis and Westlaw. For some federal legislation, I might go to Thomas [15] first. The Internet is a great place for federal agency forms and some agency publications that Lexis and Westlaw don't have. I learned a lesson about the *Federal Register*. A faculty member was being interviewed by a newspaper about new regulations that had come out that day. My patron needed them right away. I said, "Of course, I can do this." I hopped onto Lexis and tried to find them. They were not there yet. I hopped onto Westlaw and they were not there yet, either. Then I went to GPO Access [12], and there they were. I was amazed that I could get it not only for free, but much more quickly than these $100 per hour services. They put it right up the morning it comes out.

Where does the Internet fit into your overall research approach?

In terms of finding legal documents, I still turn to Lexis and Westlaw more than to the Internet, because Lexis and Westlaw are easier to search. They have an archive of data that goes way back. The Internet is not good on archiving old material. If I'm looking for a case that just came out, and it is not a U. S. Supreme Court case but from one of the federal circuits or from a state court, I might turn to the Internet to get it more quickly than Lexis or Westlaw does. The Internet can be good for keeping up with what is current. But Lexis and Westlaw are there to sell the information, so they try to get it right out there, too.

Have you had research requests you were able to fulfill by using only the Internet?

Besides that *Federal Register* example I mentioned, I am able to get publications from organizations, little pamphlets that tend not to get cataloged in libraries. Using only the Internet, I can get agency forms and other kinds of forms. A couple of years ago, the Internet was my best and sometimes my only source of legal ethics materials. The rules of professional conduct for a particular state or, more importantly, the ethics opinions of the states I could find in synopsis form elsewhere, but not in full text. More of them are showing up on Lexis and Westlaw now. The Internet has helped me tremendously in communicating with my colleagues. I can just put my question out there on our wonderful law librarians' listservs, and somebody will know the answer.

Do you use Westlaw and Lexis through their proprietary software or on the Web?

As a reference team, we use the proprietary software. I have made a push to go in through Xchange on Lexis and through the Web on Westlaw, because I feel a need to upgrade my skills so that I can teach it. I don't always have the proprietary software when I teach elsewhere. As long as you have Web access you can get to the system.

Are there differences between Web-based Westlaw or Lexis and the equivalent proprietary services that affect your preference on where to search?

It tends to take a little longer if I am going in through the Web, but not so much longer that it bothers me. If people are paying for Net time, it would be more of a factor. If you are going on in the middle of the afternoon, everything is going to take longer, whereas if you do it first thing in the morning it will be quicker.

What Internet sites do you use for legal research?

FindLaw [6] is absolutely, positively number one in my mind. If it's law and it's out there on the Web, FindLaw is going to point me to it. I find myself going to American Law Sources Online (ALSO) [4] if I'm looking for state primary authority. I like the way they have it set up. They are in the business of trying to keep it up-to-date and finding the state links. I go to Thomas all the time for federal legislation. Among subscription services on the Web, I use Congressional

Universe [44] a lot. It provides a wide variety of information published by and about Congress, including the *U. S. Code*, as well as the *Federal Register* and the *Code of Federal Regulations*. That's another example of where books might have become obsolete, because Congressional Universe does it so much better in electronic form.

What about FindLaw impresses you so much?

FindLaw impresses me in a number of ways. I like the concept of librarians finding what's out there on the Web that is related to law, and categorizing it. They are doing a great job. FindLaw is the legal version of Yahoo! [66]. I also have to tell you about customer service. With a lot of big companies, you don't get answers right away, but every time I write to FindLaw, I get a message right back. They'll answer my questions in minutes.

Do you use any generic Web search tools that are not billed as being particularly for finding the law?

I use generic search tools all the time, but not for legal research. I prefer a true directory to a search engine almost every time. I almost always start with Yahoo!. The search engines that I use are AltaVista [61], Infoseek [65], HotBot [64], and Excite [63]. I don't use metasearch tools like Dogpile [62]. I teach them but I tend not to use them.

Do you use listservs and newsgroups in connection with legal research?

I use listservs but never newsgroups. I was on some newsgroups several years ago, recreationally. The listservs draw the professional people together more than the newsgroups do, and you get a sense of community among the law librarians. You know whom you are talking to on LAW-LIB [70].

How do you deal with the volume of traffic from the listservs?

It depends on what else I'm working on at the time. If it's a very busy time for me, I delete messages without reading them. If it's not a very busy time, I'll at least look at the subject lines and who is sending the messages. If it seems like a message might be interesting, I'll take a look at it.

How do you rate the importance of listservs in your overall work?

Listservs are extremely important because that's one way to share resources and knowledge. Anybody can get out there and ask a professional question. It's part of what we do all the time. I might not know who knows the answer, but on the listservs I'm going to get that answer. The listservs traditionally have been the way I hear about good new sites for legal materials. I know there are other ways of finding out about new sites, but if it's a really good research site, they are going to talk about it on LAW-LIB.

What are some other ways to keep up with what's new on the Web?

You could go to Cornell's Big Ear [22]. They listen to LAW-LIB and some others. Big Ear tries to steer you to what is new. Another way to keep current, not only with new sites but with new issues, is *Law Library Resource Xchange* (LLRX) [1].

What triggers you to answer questions posed on listservs?

If I know something off the top of my head and I don't have to do any research, I will answer a question. There's a time factor too; I have to have had enough time to read through the messages.

How do you rate the quality and reliability of legal resources on the Internet?

I don't have as much to worry about as one might with some other disciplines, because legal resources tend to be put there by reliable organizations. Primary authority is issued by the government. It's put there by the government itself or by an educational institution. You always have to look at who's giving it to you. Is it a legitimate organization? Even if it is a legitimate organization, what are the reasons they are giving it to you? They might have a slant, and you would want to recognize that fact.

What are the main deficiencies of Internet legal resources?

The lack of any kind of significant archive of material. We started putting stuff out there in the early or mid 90s and went forward. You can't rely on the Internet for any kind of comprehensive case law research. It's just not there, unless you are focusing only on the U. S. Supreme Court. The fact that each state puts out its own material means that you can't search for a couple of states at the same time. It's all at different Web sites put out by all these different organizations. It's not collected in one place and searchable at one time.

It's like taking a Greyhound bus all around the country to get the stuff. It is an information highway, so I thought I'd throw in one highway metaphor! What are the main improvements you'd like to see in Internet legal resources?

Archives of case law would be a really good thing, to actually allow people to do case law research. Although some search engines are starting to provide a bit more flexibility, allowing sophisticated users to build good searches, they are not there yet.

They are not like Lexis and Westlaw, where you can really manipulate your search.

Who would have the resources and the reasons to provide this, a large backfile of state court opinions with cross-file searching?

The law schools would have the reason. If they had unlimited resources, they might work on that. They would see the benefit. Unless somebody got a grant, I don't see it happening.

Has there been a search where you felt sure the information had to be on the Internet and you never were able to find it?

I am in the middle of one right now. It's a Maryland Bar Association publication, a report from one of their committees. It astounds me that I am not able to find it. I still don't believe that it's not there! It's a 1998 report, so it's not too old to be there. I'm also trying to find the 1997 report from the same committee. The 1997 report shouldn't be too new.

Do you have to explain deficiencies of Internet legal research when you are teaching or talking to faculty?

Some patrons do think everything is on Web. You have to tell them "No, you are not going to find everything." A woman called me yesterday, asking where she could find the USCA on the Web. I told her you could find the USC at the House Law Library [14] and at Cornell [27]. She said, "No, no, I mean the USCA. Where is that?" She needed some convincing that you need to get on Westlaw to find the USCA.

Somehow they don't understand that the "A" is for "Annotated", and the annotations are property of

West Publishing. How do you capture and save information from the Internet?

It depends on whom I am doing it for. Often I just copy and paste into an email message, or just send them the uniform resource locator (URL) to look at. I usually do not save the research onto my hard drive.

Is the Internet affecting the role of the legal research specialist?

People appreciate us more than ever. It's never been a fear of mine that providing all this information to everybody is going to wipe out librarians and information professionals. There is so much more information out there, and people need more guidance than ever. The books in the library are all available to the patrons too, but that never meant you didn't need a reference librarian to help you find what's there.

What can patrons do when they first bring you a research request to help you do the best job?

Give me as much information about what you need as you possibly can. Think in terms of narrow, specific issues, not just broad ones. Try to be as accurate as you can with the information you've got. If you're not sure about specific details, tell me you're not sure. Don't guess and present it as if it were real.

What is it about online legal research that attracts you?

It's almost like playing a musical instrument. You practice and practice and get better and better until you're able to pull out the information you want in the most efficient way. I remember once having two computers sitting next to each other — I was doing Lexis on one and Westlaw on the other — and seeing where I could get something the quickest.

Super Searcher Secrets

- *On the path taken...*Most of the time I can make a beeline for a source. Sometimes I need some background information. If I grab a Nutshell off the reserve shelf and open it up, it is going to tell me exactly which statutes and which cases are the most important. I don't have to start with the index to the code or anything like that.

- *On the effect of budget...*It affects me a great deal in that I don't have to worry about budget at all. I have unlimited Lexis and Westlaw. Since we pay a flat rate, I don't have to worry about whether I can get on and tinker, or do the most precise search, and I don't have to worry about getting it cheaper somewhere else.

- *On obsolete hardcopy resources...*The *Index of Legal Periodicals* and the *Legal Resource Index* go back in electronic format to 1980. Any time I am looking for law review articles post-1980, I search the index online, and that makes the hardcopy indexes obsolete. The only time I open those books is if I need something more historical. Shepard's — that's a big one. I never Shepardize with books unless, of course, I am teaching somebody how to do it.

- *On preferring Lexis or Westlaw...*It's a combination of things, but content has a lot to do with it. If you want cases, Westlaw has been publishing them in the Key Number System for many decades. They are one up in case law searching, and I always turn there first. An example of the content I like better on Lexis is their federal legislation libraries and files. I turn to them first for that.

- *On when to use the Internet...*I would be looking for material that I couldn't find on Lexis and Westlaw. For some federal legislation, I might go to Thomas first. The Internet is a great place for federal agency forms and some agency publications that Lexis and Westlaw don't have. GPO Access gets the

Federal Register right up the morning it comes out. If I'm looking for a brand new case from one of the federal circuits or from a state court, I might turn to the Internet.

- *On favorite Internet sites...*FindLaw is absolutely, positively number one in my mind. If it's law and it's out there on the Web, FindLaw is going to point me to it. I find myself going to American Law Sources Online (ALSO) if I'm looking for state primary authority. Among subscription services on the Web, I go to Congressional Universe a lot.

- *On ways to keep current with Internet legal resources...*You could go to Cornell's Big Ear. They listen to LAW-LIB and some others. Big Ear tries to steer you to what is new. Another way to keep current, not only with new sites but with new issues, is *Law Library Resource Xchange* (LLRX).

- *On the Internet's effect on the role of the legal research specialist...*People appreciate us more than ever. It's never been a fear of mine that providing all this information to everybody is going to wipe out librarians and information professionals. There is so much more information out there, and people need more guidance than ever.

Leigh C. Webber

Teaching Old Dogs New Tricks

Leigh C. Webber has practiced law, has taught law school courses about computers and the law, and presents continuing legal education seminars on Internet legal research around the United States and Canada. Mr. Webber has taught over 8,000 attorneys in dozens of Continuing Legal Education (CLE) seminars for state bar associations and other CLE organizations.

lwebber@knowhow.com
www.knowhow.com/

You teach a continuing legal education seminar called "Using the Internet for Legal Research." How did you get started with that?

I've made a career over the last ten years of teaching continuing legal education seminars to attorneys across the country. I have taught various topics, most of them technology-related. As the Internet became more popular and attorneys became more curious about it, I started getting lots of questions in my classes about its possibilities for legal research. So I spent a lot of time exploring it, using it in that way, and figuring out how to explain it to people who understand law practice and legal research using conventional methods. I don't make my living by actually doing research day-to-day. I do online legal research for the sake of being able to consult and teach. People who take my class sometimes take advantage of my offer to ask me for help if they need it with a particular project or question. I get involved in that way, but I don't do consulting work as a researcher.

Who is your audience, and what is the primary objective of the seminar?

The courses are advertised to attorneys. Most of the people who come are attorneys, and they earn CLE (continuing legal education) credit for attending. About ten percent of the audience spends all their time doing legal research as law librarians, research paralegals or something like that. They are accustomed to doing legal research in the conventional way and they are good at it. They are curious and want to learn the opportunities and shortcomings of using the Internet for legal research. People in the legal profession are not technology experts. They are not computer experts, and don't care to become computer experts. I've developed a way to bridge that gap, to help them with that transition. My course is not like ones in legal research *per se*. It's a course in legal research on the Internet. Most of those who attend are attorneys from smaller to mid-sized firms doing legal research themselves.

Are there some common preconceptions about the Internet among attorneys who attend your seminars?

People learn differently, so I find different areas of awareness and lack of awareness. Some of the preconceptions I commonly encounter are about the source of materials, coverage, and the organization of the Internet. Some are unaware of where the information actually comes from. They don't know who provides it, and they don't know the implications of collections of material put together by volunteers or amateurs, as contrasted with ones assembled by librarians or by agencies responsible for creating the information in the first place. People often think that everything is available on the Internet. Whatever they want, they think it ought to be there. If there is a case from 1968, it ought to be available on the Internet. If there is a state statute, it ought to be available on the Internet. They are surprised to find that is not the case. The biggest difficulty people have is getting their head around the chaos of the

Net. You walk into a law library and it even smells organized. Everything is arranged and there is a smiling person to help you to find the right aisles and materials. On the Net there are no neat rows of shelves and books arranged with numbers stamped on the spines in ascending order. It becomes frustrating. People stare at the screen and have no idea how to proceed.

Those are preconceptions with negative consequences. Are there some with positive ones?

Attorneys largely think of Internet research in terms of the kinds of the things they have conventionally done with legal research. If you think of the Internet as just a replacement for that, you are missing an enormous part of its value. There are things that are very useful for attorneys that aren't conventional law materials, nor would you find them in a conventional law library. Take a personal injury case as an example. You're concerned about things like medical evidence, traffic patterns and the timing of the light at the intersection. What on earth is this medical report that is full of jargon? Did the person conducting the medical examination do a good job? Is there any way I can pick this thing apart? There is a Web site that focuses on anatomy, *Wheeless' Textbook of Orthopaedics* [Wheeless.Belgianorthoweb.be/med/htm] [102, see Appendix A]. The home page is made up mostly of a large skeleton. When you move your mouse over it carefully, you can click on a part of the body and get information related to that part. An attorney may not know the name of the bone, but knowing where it is, he can get information about that part of the body. The information might include x-rays, other types of medical imaging, examples, and descriptions of the kinds of examinations conducted when considering an injury to that part of the body. It answers a number of questions, such as what are the tests someone takes, what do the tests mean, what are the differential diagnosis factors that a physician would use and what are other kinds of problems in diagnosis and treatment? It's wonderful. You can look at all the things the orthopedic surgeon in your case has said she or he has done, and then, at this Web site, see what those things mean, what things weren't done and the opinions or issues that some of the best medical minds in the world have come up with.

If you are dealing with a car accident, you might want to find out how many similar accidents have happened with that kind of vehicle, or how many accidents have happened on this stretch of highway compared with other highways. Is there something wrong with the roadway or the way the highway was engineered? That is something you wouldn't find in a conventional law library. Information like that is maintained by various federal agencies and insurance organizations on the Net. If you look at legal research like this—legal research means finding out stuff that helps you help your client—it includes a much broader range of things than what the statutes and cases say. The wider view opens you to a far more useful pursuit on the Internet than the black-letter law pursuit, which is largely frustrating and unsatisfactory.

Do you feel the research of law *per se* on the Internet is largely frustrating?

It depends on the kind of law. For most practical purposes, there are a couple of major limitations that render it pretty quickly not unusable but—let me put it this way—you have to use it in a different way. For example, on the commercial online services, the digests are an important tool. Digests are created when some thoughtful person has read the case, condensed it and organized a collection of those condensations topically. Outside of the Web versions of service like Westlaw [60] and Lexis [54], that type of thing is not available on the Net at all.

Let's focus on statute law and case law. In some states there is no online collection of statutes at all. None! For the states that do have online collections, are they kept up to date? Is there any easy way to find out if the section of the statute you are looking at has been amended? You have to consider whether you can find session laws someplace and look those things up. Those are sometimes kept separately, they are organized separately, and you need different search technologies to work with them.

Then you have to correlate pieces of that to where it would be found in the code because, in the process of codification, things get arranged differently.

You bet! There are so many little frustrations. When you open any law book, like a consolidation of statutes, in the very front there is a statement that "This represents the laws in force as of" and then a date. That's critically important. The question is not whether a statute collection is out of date. They're *all* out of date. The question is *how* out of date it is. How far back do I have to check the session laws to know that I've overlapped this collection? In statute resources on the Internet, it's rare that the Web site will say, "This consolidation represents the laws in force as of such-and-such a date." It just doesn't say. Now what do you do? Some states are lucky enough to have all their laws in effect on the same day. But in many states that is not the case, and laws take effect from time to time throughout the year.

How do people look up statutes? There are two ways. In one case, you know the statute is there and you want to read it. In the other case, you are wondering if there is a statute. In the first case, the Internet can be wonderful. You navigate through a series of menus — the titles, chapters and sections — scroll down to the subsection and read it. What if you don't know whether there is a statute? That's a far more difficult problem. What if you want to know if there are any federal programs for housing assistance for elderly persons? In the main table of contents of the *United States Code*, none of the titles says "Housing Programs for Elderly Persons." Which title are you going to open up? You have the entire collection! It's under "Banks and Banking - Title XIII." When you open up Title XIII, you find that one of the chapters has to do with national housing. Underneath that, you'll find — if you know where to scroll to — that, yes, there are in fact federal programs for housing assistance for elderly persons. Many people in my classes have the misconception that you look it up in some kind of search engine. You "search" for something. You search for elderly persons or housing programs for the elderly or senior citizens or some other futile thing like that. They have tried that. They are totally frustrated because it doesn't work. The reason is, although there may be a table of contents to Internet statute collections, there is no index in the conventional sense that you would find in the printed books. There is no such thing in most places on the Internet, so people try full-text searching. They discover the enormous problem of full-text searching on Internet legal resources. The problem is, you can't find words that aren't in the statutes. Unfortunately, you can only find the words the legislators have used.

Let's bring in an example here.

I was teaching a class in Minnesota at a time when I knew, because I lived in Minnesota, that the legislature was considering a bill to ban ATM surcharges. We are all familiar with the phenomenon of being charged $1.00 or $1.50 for using an automated teller machine if it's not one that is operated by your own bank. So Minnesota, with its fine social conscience, introduced legislation to ban ATM surcharges. It was in the news. I knew it was there. Minnesota has a very good online statute, bill, and legislative information site [20]. It is one of the best, if not the best, in the country. So I thought it would be easy. I searched for ATM and I found it. Do you know what ATM means? ATM means "asynchronized transfer mode." That is a telecommunications technology. "ATM" was in a bill somewhere because they were talking about some kind of standards or whether the Public Service Commission would regulate

ATM technology. I couldn't find anything about banking machines or cash machines or teller machines or automated teller machines. I tried all kinds of things — like "autom* teller." Finally I went through every session law and looked at the titles of each one. Minnesota makes a lot of laws every year — something like 2,000 a session — and I read through the titles of every one until I found one that looked likely. Then I discovered what my problem was. It was my stupidity. You see, I should have looked up "electronic funds transfer device" and I would have found the bill instantly. If you don't know the words the legislators used, you can't find things. That's a huge problem in using conventional means. You can't approach finding laws you are not aware of, using the kinds of things you would conventionally and normally think of, like looking up indexes that don't exist. A service like Westlaw has what librarians call a controlled vocabulary. You look in the index to find what term in the controlled vocabulary is appropriate for your search. West's system uses its Key Numbers. There is nothing like that in Internet statute and case law searching.

What suggestions can you make for overcoming that limitation?

One of the best ways to find federal laws, regulations, and even cases in some situations is to go to the Web site of the federal agency that is responsible for it. Federal agencies are under a mandate called the Paperwork Reduction Act, which requires them to make their information available to the public in electronic form as economically as possible. It doesn't mandate any Web sites, but it turns out that the Internet is the only practical way to give effect to the mandate. Some federal agency Web sites have collections of law-related material including links straight into the portions of the *United States Code* that they are responsible for, or that control their area of operation. Some link to regulations. That is fabulous, because the *Code of Federal Regulations* has an unusable table of contents. It goes down to the title and then section. It's too gross and doesn't give you the kind of precision you need to locate a regulation. You are faced with full-text searching, which is just a joke because there are so many of them. Some federal agency sites have links to cases, too. So it helps to think, "What are the organizations on the Internet that would give me the information, or point to it?" In a law library, everything is in one big room. The Internet is in a million tiny rooms. A lawyer never would have thought of flying to Washington, D.C., going to the office of the Equal Employment Opportunity Commission, walking into its reading room and finding on the shelves a book that lists the regulations the EEOC administers. But that's exactly what you do on the Internet.

Besides federal agencies, what kinds of organizations might enable this approach?

State agencies, professional organizations, trade associations and special-interest groups. If you're interested, for example, in employment law, besides federal and state agencies, labor unions have Web sites. You explore the site and you find, wow, here's a collection of statute references or regulations or cases or commentaries. There may be a position paper. Of course position papers might give their spin, but many of them provide useful discussion and references. Some state agency Web sites include their regulatory hearings and findings on administrative review hearings, which are very difficult to find even in a good law library.

Can you make any generalizations about the path you follow on the Internet?

If the question relates primarily to federal matters, I might start with a couple of the legal encyclopedias, like the one at Cornell [27]. That's organized topically, like a conventional encyclopedia. Then I'd look for federal agencies. If the question involves state law or private law, it's more difficult. It would depend on the state. If it were a state that has well-organized agency resources, that might be a useful approach. Often a more useful one is going to a major mega-collection like FindLaw [6] or Hieros Gamos [7]. FindLaw is currently my favorite collection of bookmarks [96]. I said the Internet in general is not like walking into a law library where you have organized rows of shelves, but FindLaw kind of is that. You can travel down different series of menus that are organized in a way I think many attorneys find intuitive. You work your way through those bookmark collections until you find references to the kind of material that would be helpful. So FindLaw often is a good starting place. For international law I prefer Hieros Gamos. It depends on the nature of the question. Say somebody asks, "What are the export and import restrictions on yogurt?" In FindLaw you're probably not going to drill down to something under Y for yogurt. That search would take a different approach from a question like, "What are grandparents' access rights in the State of Minnesota?" The approach for each has to be different.

You're going to spend a lot of time wandering around. If you organize your own bookmarks, you will answer this problem over time. You'll discover what resources are most useful for the kind of work you do. Different practices areas, different personal styles, different delegation approaches, different staffing arrangements — all affect the way someone uses the Internet. Most attorneys, even in general practices, tend to concentrate on particular areas of practice rather than being true generalists. To the extent that you specialize, it becomes easier to develop your own collection of bookmarks.

Besides FindLaw and Hieros Gamos, what are some sites you commonly use?

There are a couple of dozen that I call major legal sites. Two that are worth looking into deeply are The Internet Legal Resource

Guide [8] and the Legal Information Institute (LII) at Cornell [27]. LII has the fingerprints of law librarians all over it, which I love. It lacks a little bit of visual punch and you have to spend some time exploring it.

There's a difference between a directory or catalog and a search engine. Can you make any general statements about when you gravitate toward using one or the other?

At the beginning of a project, often it is more helpful to start with a catalog, and my favorite catalog is my own. I stress that everybody ought to organize his or her own bookmarks like a catalog. Then go to the catalogs online like FindLaw. If you still feel there is material you haven't been able to find that way, then use a search engine, but use the ones focusing on law before trying a general-purpose search engine. I almost never begin a project with a general search engine.

What should searchers do when they find a relevant document at a site?

When you find something useful, don't simply read it and then go back to your hit list. If they have one page that is useful, they may have a whole bunch of others. You need to explore the Web site. A hit in a search engine might be to a secondary page. Regrettably, a lot of law-related Web sites are done by people who know the law but may not be gifted Web site designers. Often there is no back link to the site's home page or to the page logically preceding the one you're reading. If you learn what a uniform resource locator (URL) is, you can explore the site. You can remove the trailing parts of the URL progressively, slash by slash, to reach higher levels of the site's organization or its home page.

Are there other browser tricks searchers can use to help their research?

There are different mechanical skills in using a Web browser that people need to understand. Using the right mouse button rather than the left one to click on a link will produce a shortcut menu. One of the items on the shortcut menu is "Open in New Window," which means the document at that link, instead of replacing the content of the current browser window, will launch another Web browser window containing the document the link refers to. That lets you go back and forth between two browser windows and look at both pages at once if you like. You might want to have the statute up in one window and the case in the other, and not have to constantly hit the back button and the forward button and waste the time it takes to reload those pages. It also lets you explore hit lists much more effectively. In a new window, you can wander around the designated Web site and, when you're done, you don't have to hit the Back button a dozen times to return to your hit list. You simply close the window and your hit list is still in its original window waiting for you to go to the next place.

Newer versions of Web browsers have a "More Like This" button. When you find a highly relevant page and click on that button, it takes the contents of the page you are looking at and submits them to a search engine to find other pages that match it. It's something like the way the Excite [63] search engine works. When you find a helpful document in the Excite hit list, there's a button or link that says, "Search for more documents like this one." That only works if you have used Excite to produce the hit list. The newer Web browsers, no matter how you worked your way to a particular page — whether it was through a catalog, one of your existing bookmarks, a general purpose search engine, or someone gave you a URL — you can click the "More Like This" button. The results have a better signal-to-noise ratio than most people would achieve doing a search themselves with a general search engine.

That allows you to use the hit list as a hub and "spoke out" to the sites that it mentions.

I love the way you put that — using it as a hub with spokes. I'm going to use that in my next class because I think it's a nice metaphor to show people what's really going on.

When you find a great page, what do you do with it? Are we just stuck with File Save As and remembering to save the graphics?

There are three or four different things that you might want to do. One is File Save As. It can be awkward later if someone opens one of those pages in their word processor. If you saved it as hypertext markup language (HTML), it might be time-consuming to load it into a word processor. You can save it as raw text. You select it in the Web browser window, copy it and then paste it into a word processor document. You'll often get a better outcome that way than with File Save As. If you want the whole document, pressing Ctrl-A in your Web browser will instantly select the entire page no matter how many screens long it is. Then pressing Ctrl-C will copy it and, switching to your word processor, pressing Ctrl-V will paste it there. On a Mac, it's Command-A, Command-C, and Command-V.

You can send the link or the document by email. That can be helpful if you are doing research away from your own computer. You may be at a walk-up computer in a law library where bookmarking or saving would do no good, since the information would be stored on that computer and not be available to you later. You can email the page or the link to yourself at your email address and pick it up when you get back to your own computer. You also could send it to your client. When sending to someone other than yourself, you might want to send the link instead of the page. Sending a page by email produces what could be a gigantic attachment to an email message. That might be pretty slow to download when you have to access your email over a modem. Clients do not appreciate getting two-megabyte emails from their attorneys. It's bad manners. You can send a link by email. It's very, very short. They can click it and go look at it in their own browser when they choose, without being forced to wait for it to download in email.

How can legal searchers best take advantage of what the Web does offer as a research environment?

Be open to serendipity. Say you are looking for one thing and you stumble onto something else that might not be useful for the project you are working on, but might be very useful for other purposes later. Be open to exploiting those things. That's something that doesn't happen very much in conventional research. It happens on the Net all the time. It could be a great way to waste tons of hours in an activity commonly called surfing. But if you are not open to that, at least a little bit, you might waste many, many hours online at a later date. If you can take advantage of the little nuggets you stumble onto and keep them organized, it can save you time later. Say you are looking up something under child custody and access. You find a page that is not very helpful to the exact question you are researching now. You notice that the page is put together by an organization devoted to the step-parenting role. Besides that document, they have a collection of resources for stepparents. Are you a family law lawyer? Are you likely to need that later? Even in your current case, is your job simply providing answers to legal questions? Maybe that site would be helpful for your client. It may have information that is more helpful to your client in the long run than the particular interlocutory application you currently are making.

Super Searcher Secrets

- *On common preconceptions about the Internet...*Some of the preconceptions I commonly encounter are about the source of materials, coverage, and the organization of the Internet. Some are unaware of where the information actually comes from. People often think that everything is available on the Internet. The biggest difficulty people have is getting their head around the chaos of the Net.

- *On the date of materials...*When you open any law book, like a consolidation of statutes, in the very front there is a statement that "This represents the laws in force as of" and then a date. The question is not whether a statute collection is out of date. They *all* are out of date. The question is *how* out of date it is. How far back do I have to check the session laws to know that I've overlapped this collection? In statute resources on the Internet, it's rare that the Web site will say.

- *On the problem of statute research on the Web...*What if you want to know if there are any federal programs for housing assistance for elderly persons? In the main table of contents of the *United States Code,* none of the titles says "Housing Programs for Elderly Persons." Which title are you going to open up? Many people think you look it up in some kind of search engine. They are totally frustrated because it doesn't work. In Internet statute collections, there is no index in the conventional sense that you would find in the printed books.

- *On overcoming the problem of statute research on the Web...*Some federal agency Web sites have collections of law-related material including links straight into the portions of the *United States Code* that they are responsible for, or that control their area of operation. Some link to regulations. That is fabulous because the *Code of Federal Regulations* has an unusable table of contents. Sometimes their sites have links to cases, too.

- *On what makes FindLaw useful to attorneys...*The Internet is not like walking into a law library where you have organized rows of shelves, but FindLaw kind of is that. You can travel down different series of menus that are organized in a way I think many attorneys find intuitive. You work your way through those bookmark collections until you find references to the kind of material that would be helpful.
- *On using Internet bookmarks, directories and search engines...* At the beginning of a project, often it is more helpful to start with a catalog, and my favorite catalog is my own. I stress that everybody ought to organize his or her own bookmarks like a catalog. Then go to the catalogs online like FindLaw. If you still feel there is material you haven't been able to find that way, then use a search engine, but use the ones focusing on law before trying a general-purpose search engine.
- *On exploring Web sites...*When you find something useful, don't simply read it and then go back to your hit list. If they have one page that is useful, they may have a whole bunch of others. You need to explore the Web site. If you learn what a URL is, you can explore the site. You can remove the trailing parts of the URL progressively, slash by slash, to reach higher levels of the site's organization or its home page.
- *On using Web browsers effectively with hit lists...*Using the right mouse button rather than the left one to click on a link in a hit list lets you open the hit page in a new browser window. You can wander around the designated Web site in the new window and, when you're done, you don't have to hit the Back button a dozen times to return to your hit list.

Appendix A:
Referenced Internet Resources

Webzines

1. *Law Library Resource Xchange*
   www.llrx.com/

Legal Research Guidance Sites

2. *Best Guide to Canadian Legal Research*
   www.LegalResearch.org/
3. *The Virtual Chase*
   www.virtualchase.com/

Legal Catalogs, Directories, and Search Engines

4. American Law Sources Online (ALSO)
   www.lawsource.com/also/
5. CataLaw
   www.catalaw.com/
6. FindLaw
   www.findlaw.com/
7. Hieros Gamos
   www.hg.org
8. Internet Legal Resource Guide
   www.ilrg.com/
9. Law Crawler
   www.lawcrawler.com/

10. Law Runner
    www.lawrunner.com/

Federal Government Sites

11. EDGAR Database of Corporate Information
    www.sec.gov/edgarhp.htm
12. GPO Access
    www.access.gpo.gov
13. Internet Grateful Med
    igm.nlm.nih.gov/
14. Internet Law Library (U.S. House of Representatives)
    law.house.gov/
15. Thomas
    thomas.loc.gov
16. U.S. Bureau of Prisons FOIA
    www.bop.gov/ogcpg/ogcfoia.html
17. U.S. Department of Justice, Civil Division
    www.usdoj.gov/civil/civil.html
18. U.S. Department of Justice, Civil Division,
    Frequently Requested FOIA-Processed Records
    www.usdoj.gov/crt/foia/records.htm
19. U.S. Environmental Protection Agency
    www.epa.gov/

State Government Sites

20. Minnesota House of Representatives
    www.house.leg.state.mn.us/
21. New Jersey State Legislature
    www.njleg.state.nj.us/

Academic Sites

22. Big Ear
    barratry.law.cornell.edu:5123/notify/buzz.html
23. The Center for Information Law and Policy (Villanova)
    www.law.vill.edu/

24. Federal Web Locator
www.law.vill.edu/Fed-Agency/fedwebloc.html
25. InSITE
128.253.118.14:8080/insite/insitetp.html
26. JURIST: The Law Professors' Network (University of Pittsburgh School of Law)
www.jurist.law.pitt.edu/
27. Legal Information Institute (LII; Cornell Law School)
www.law.cornell.edu/
28. Meta-Index for U.S. Legal Research
gsulaw.gsu.edu/metaindex/
29. WashLaw WEB
www.washlaw.edu/
30. World Wide Web Virtual Law Library
www.law.indiana.edu/law/v-lib/lawindex.html

American Bar Association

31. ABA Network (American Bar Association)
www.abanet.org/
32. ABA Site-tation
www.abanet.org/LAWLINK/site-tation.html

Canadian, Australian, and British Courts and Case Law Sites

33. Australasian Legal Information Institute (AustLII)
www.austlii.edu.au/
34. British Columbia Court of Appeal
www.courts.gov.bc.ca/CA/Ca-main.htm
35. British Columbia Supreme Court
www.courts.gov.bc.ca/SC/Sc-main.htm
36. eCarswell
www.carswell.com/ecarswell/index.html
37. Casebase
www.smithbernal.com/casebase_frame.htm
38. Societe quebecoise d'information juridique (SOQUIJ)
www.soquij.qc.ca/
39. Supreme Court of Canada
www.scc-csc.gc.ca/

40. Supreme Court of Canada opinions
 www.droit.umontreal.ca/doc/csc-scc/en/index.html
41. Virtual Canadian Law Library
 www.droit.umontreal.ca/doc/biblio/en/index.html

Commercial Services

42. Bureau of National Affairs, Inc.
 www.bna.com/
43. CDB Infotek
 www.cdb.com/public/
44. Congressional Universe
 www.cispubs.com/conguniv/welcome.htm
45. CourtLink
 www.courtlink.com/
46. CaseStream
 MarketSpan Online
 www.marketspan.com
47. Commerce Clearing House (CCH)
 toolkit.cch.com/
48. Dialog
 www.dialog.com/
49. Dow Jones Interactive
 www.djinteractive.com
50. Dun & Bradstreet
 www.dnb.com

 Duns Legal Search
 www.dnb-dc.com/dnbngovt/legalsearch.html
51. Integrated Health Services, Inc. (IHS)
 www.ihs-inc.com
52. Global Access
 www.disclosure.com/dga/
53. LEGI-SLATE
 www.legislate.com
54. Lexis-Nexis
 www.lexis-nexis.com/
55. LOIS
 www.pita.com/

56. Martindale-Hubbell
www.martindale.com/
57. PACER (Public Access to Court Electronic Records)
www.dcd.uscourts.gov/pacer.html
58. QuickLaw
www.qlsys.ca/
59. VersusLaw
www.versuslaw.com/
60. Westlaw
www.westlaw.com/

General Catalogs, Directories, Search Engines, and Metasearch Engines

61. AltaVista
http://www.altavista.com/
62. Dogpile
www.dogpile.com/
63. Excite
www.excite.com/
64. HotBot
www.hotbot.com/
65. InfoSeek
www.infoseek.com/
66. Yahoo!
www.yahoo.com/

Listservs

67. CALL-L@unb.ca (Canadian Association of Law Libraries / Association canadienne des bibliotheques de droit; discussion list focusing on law librarianship in Canada;
Send the following message to listserv@unb.ca or listserv@listserv.unb.ca or call-l-server@unb.ca:
subscribe CALL-L Your Name
see CALL/ACBD InfoPages at www.callacbd.ca/ or listserv.unb.ca/archives/call-l.html
68. CLRN-L@world.mmltd.com (listserv sponsored by Canadian Legal Research Network for discussion of issues relevant to the legal research undertaking within law firms, corporate legal departments, and independent research units, including the role and practice of research specialists; the relationship between research lawyers and other professionals; the means of evaluating the economic efficiencies

of centralized research and retrieval; and the creation and maintenance of legal research databases containing the work product of lawyers.) To subscribe send an email message to: majordomo@world.mmltd.com with the following in the body of the message: subscribe CLRN-L myname@domain (Note: replace the word "myname@domain" with your actual e-mail address.) Commands in the subject line are not processed. (related Web page at http://www.notinprint.com/lrn/index.htm)

69. GOVDOC-L@LISTS.PSU.EDU (A discussion forum about government information and the Federal Depository Library program. Most subscribers are librarians, although many private and public information producers are represented as well.)
    Send the following message to LISTSERV@LISTS.PSU.EDU:
    SUB GOVDOC-L Yourfirstname Yourlastname
    (User Guide at www.staff.uiuc.edu/~raeann/govdoc-l.html)
70. LAW-LIB@vuw.ac.nz (New Zealand-based Law Librarians Group discussion list; includes announcements about meetings, seminars, conferences, discussions about publishers, etc.)
    Send the following message to majordomo@vuw.ac.nz:
    subscribe law-lib <your email address>
    (related page at www.knowledge-basket.co.nz/nzllg/welcome.html)
71. LAWLIBREF-L@lawlib.wuacc.edu (Law Library Reference; questions and issues list for legal reference librarians)
    Send the following message to listserv@lawlib.wuacc.edu: subscribe lawlibref-L your firstname lastname (related page at http://lawlibdns.wuacc.edu/archive.html and http://public.1jextra.com/mailinglists/wwwlawlibref-1/index.html) (related page at http://lawlib.wuacc.edu/) (related page at http://www.washlaw.edu/listserv.html)
72. LAWSRC-L@listserv.law.cornell.edu (National daily moderated Internet legal resource list for exchange of information about Internet law resources for teachers, librarians, lawyers; was archived at http://users.aol.com/abiaca/lawsrc.htm; seems to be turning into mostly a legal news distribution list
    Send the following message to listserv@listserv.law.cornell.edu:
    subscribe lawsrc-L Your full name
    (archives at www.rwneill.com/lawsrc.htm and mailmunch.law.cornell.edu/mhonarc/LAWSRC/ and www.legalminds.org/listsaver/lawsrc-l/ and //www.reference.com/)
73. LAWTECH@abanet.org (American Bar Association list for discussion of legal-related technology used in law practices and courts, such as software, hardware, use of the Internet, etc.; includes Legal Technology Resource Center (LTRC) announcements)
    Send the following message to listserv@abanet.org:
    subscribe lawtech Your Name
    (related page at http://www.abanet.org/ and archives at mail.abanet.org/discussions/archives/lawtech/)
74. LawTech@complaw.com (Law Office Technology; discussions related to hardware and software; also LawTech-Digest)

Send a message to lawtech-request@complaw.com with the subject: subscribe (see www.complaw.com/cgi-bin/lwgate/LAWTECH and www.complaw.com/cgi-bin/lwgate/LAWTECH-DIGEST)

75. NET-LAWYERS@peach.ease.lsoft.com (Lawyers and the Internet; moderated list for lawyers, librarians, law professors, paralegals, law students, and others interested in law to discuss issues related to the use of the Internet in the study, practice, development, and marketing of law; includes announcements of and questions on legal resources on the Internet.
Send the following message to listserv@peach.ease.lsoft.com:
subscribe net-lawyers Your Name
(related page at www.net-lawyers.org/; archived at
eva.dc.lsoft.com/Archives/net-lawyers.html
and ftplaw.wuacc.edu/listproc/net-lawyers/ (old to 12/96)
and www.ljextra.com/forumpages/netlawyers.html
(or www.ljx.com/mailinglists/netlaw2/) and
www.legalminds.org/listsaver/net-lawyers/)
(related page at lawlibdns.wuacc.edu/archive.html)

76. NETTRAIN@listserv.acsu.buffalo.edu (Internet/BITNET Network Trainers Discussion List. Note: Not for beginners ; HELP-NET at LISTSERV@TEMPLEVM.BITNET or LISTSERV@VM.TEMPLE.EDU or the Usenet newsgroup, bit.listserv.help-net, is for beginning users of the Internet.
Send the following message to listserv@listserv.acsu.buffalo.edu:
subscribe nettrain Your Name
(archives at listserv.acsu.buffalo.edu/archives/nettrain.html
and gatewayed to the Usenet newsgroup, bit.listserv.nettrain)

77. NETWORK2D-L@austin.onu.edu (American Bar Association list for discussion of issues raised in Network 2d, the quarterly newsletter on using technology in law offices and in the courts; lawyers)
Send the following message to listserv@austin.onu.edu:
subscribe network2d-L Your Name
(include your occupation in the subject line)
(related page at www.abanet.org/)

78. PRIVATELAWLIB-L@lawlib.wuacc.edu (Private Law Libraries list; law firms; American Association of Law Libraries Special Interest Section)
Send the following message to listserv@lawlib.wuacc.edu:
subscribe privatelawlib-L your firstname lastname
(related page at http://lawlibdns.wuacc.edu/archive.html and
http://www.aallnet.org/discuss/ - see PLL-SIS list)

79. The TechnoLawyer Listserver (Legal Technology Discussion–for attorneys, paralegals, consultants, software developers, and interested others; ListMaster is Neil J. Squillante at nsquillante@netsquire.com)
Send the following message to commands@technolawyer.com:

subscribe listserver
(or use web-based subscription form at www.technolawyer.com/)

80. WEB4LIB-L@library.berkeley.edu (WebPAC design; Internet, World Wide Web, cataloging, electronic publishing, librarians, computing services; information technology; online public access catalogs (OPACS); web authoring)
Send the following message to listserv@library.berkeley.edu:
subscribe web4lib-l Your Name
(archives at sunsite.berkeley.edu/Web4Lib/archive.html)

Newspapers and Television

81. *Chicago Tribune*
www.chicago.tribune.com/

82. CNN
www.cnn.com/

83. *The Internet Lawyer*
internetlawyer.com/

84. *Los Angeles Times*
www.latimes.com/HOME/

85. *The New York Times*
www.nytimes.com/

86. *The Washington Post*
www.washingtonpost.com/

Professional Journals

87. *EContent* (formerly *Database*)
www.ecmag.net/

88. *Law Journal EXTRA*
www.ljx.com/contents.html

89. *Online*
www.onlineinc.com/onlinemag/index.html

90. *Searcher*
www.infotoday.com/searcher/default.htm

Miscellaneous

91. American Law Institute
www.ali.org/

92. Best's Legal Bookmarks
    www.LegalResearch.org/docs/bookmark.html
93. Books and Periodicals Online
    (Library Technology Alliances, Nuchine Nobari, ed.)
    www.periodicals.net/ or periodicals.net/
94. Fulltext Sources Online
    www.infotoday.com/fso/
95. Internet Strategies for the Paralegal in Minnesota:
    A Paralegal's Guide to the Information Super-Highway
    www.tc.umn.edu/nlhome/m212/g-jack/lrweb/lrweb.htm
96. Leigh Webber's Bookmarks
    www.knowhow.com/Research.htm
97. NAREIT Online
    www.nareit.com/
98. Online Computer Library Center (OCLC)
    homer.prod.oclc.org/
99. Research Libraries Information Network (RLIN)
    www.rlg.org/rlin.html
100. Ulrich's International Periodicals Directory
    http://www.ulrichsweb.com/ulrichs/index.html
101. University of Toronto Alphabetical Listing of Electronic Journals
    www.law-lib.utoronto.ca/resources/journals.htm
102. Wheeless' Textbook of Orthopaedics
    Wheeless.Belgianorthoweb.be/med.htm

Software

103. Alexa
    www.alexa.com/
104. PREMISE Research Software
    www.westgroup.com/products/software/premise/

Appendix B:
Glossary

This glossary includes terms used in the interviews, but is not a general or comprehensive glossary of legal research terms.

administrative regulation. In American law, rules promulgated by administrative agencies that implement, explain, enforce or carry out statutes and executive orders.

American Digest System. An extensive set of books published by West Publishing Company as an aid to finding case law. These books divide the law into topics and analytically outline the topics, assigning West Key Numbers to each topic and subtopic. Under each topic, subtopic and Key Number, the books present small, one-paragraph summaries of points decided in reported opinions of the courts. These digest paragraphs are written by West and correspond to the "headnotes" that accompany the opinions in West's case reporters. The digest system follows West's reporter system. On a national level, the American Digest System has three units with varying coverage according to time: the *Century Digest*, *Decennial Digests*, and the *General Digest*. Regional digests cover the jurisdictions in each corresponding regional reporter series, e.g., the *Pacific Digests* cover cases reported in the *Pacific Reporter*. *The Federal Digest* covers West's reporters of federal cases.

American Jurisprudence, Second Edition **(Am.Jur.2d).** A legal encyclopedia published by Lawyer's Co-operative Publishing Company that covers American law on a national scale. See "(legal) encyclopedia."

***American Law Reports* (ALR), ALR annotation.** A set of books published by Lawyer's Co-operative Publishing Company that reports the complete text of selected court opinions with annotations. Editors select cases they believe are leading or important cases. In these books, the term "annotation" has a special meaning. Rather than simple notes to the reported cases, an ALR annotation is an article or research paper providing extensive commentary on the main issue addressed in the reported case. An annotation attempts to collect, summarize and analyze other cases on the issue.

annotated code. A statutory code (see "code, codify, codification") with annotations following each section. The annotations may include the legislative history of the section, cross references to related sections, references to other research material relevant to the section, and case references and summaries for court decisions that consider the section.

authority. A statement of law by a source to which the courts give weight. See "primary authority" and "secondary authority."

Auto-Cite. An online case citator. See "citator."

British Columbia Appeal Cases. A Maritime Law Books reporter covering full text of decisions of the British Columbia Court of Appeal since June 1991.

Bureau of National Affairs, Inc. (BNA). A publisher of print and electronic news and information, reporting on developments in health care, business, labor relations, law, economics, taxation, environmental protection, safety, and other public policy and regulatory issues. BNA produces more than 200 news and information services and numerous dailies.

Canadian Abridgment. A comprehensive Canadian research tool published by Carswell and consisting of the Key and Research Guide, the General Index, the Consolidated Table of Cases, Canadian Case Digests, Canadian Current Law, Canadian Case Citations, Canadian Statute Citations, Annual Legislation, and the Index to Canadian Legal Literature. The Abridgment also includes Words and Phrases Judicially Defined in Canadian Courts and Tribunals.

CDB Infotek. A commercial online service providing access to public records information. The information is used by law firms, private investigators, insurance investigators, police, government agencies and others for such purposes as: finding people and businesses in the U. S., identifying and verifying the assets of a person or business, developing background information on a person or business, investigating insurance claims and subrogation cases, conducting pre-trial preparation.

Century Digest. A unit of the American Digest System that gives paragraph summaries of the court opinions of most appellate, state and federal courts and some lower state and federal courts. See "American Digest System."

citator. A citator is a book or online resource containing lists of citations. Citators serve several purposes. A case citator lets a researcher verify the accuracy of a citation, lets a researcher find parallel citations where the cited case is reported in alternate case reporters, lets a researcher trace the history of a case, lets a researcher assess the current validity of a case by providing a list of subsequent cases that have cited the case being checked, whether those cases follow it, reverse it, explain it, distinguish it, modify it, etc. Statute citators serve similar purposes; they verify the accuracy of a citation, may give the session law citation, amendments, replacements, or additions to the statute. See "Shepard's (Shepardize)," "Auto-Cite," "InstaCite," "KeyCite," and "QuickCite."

civil law systems. Legal systems highly influenced by Roman law characterized by statutory codes and a great reliance upon the influence of academic lawyers to develop the law.

***Code of Federal Regulations* (CFR).** An extensive set of pamphlets containing many of the regulations of federal agencies arranged in the form of a code. See "administrative regulation" and "code, codify, codification."

code, codify, codification. As bills pass through the stages of the legislative process and are enacted into law, they are published in books called Session Laws, Acts and Resolves, and Statutes at Large in more or less chronological order. Codification is the subsequent process of reorganizing, rearranging and reassembling statutes according to subject matter or topics. The codified statutes may be called a code, revision or consolidation. In a similar manner, administrative regulations originally appear in more or less chronological order in publications such as the *Federal Register* and usually are codified into an administrative code.

Commerce Clearing House (CCH). A publisher of loose-leaf services containing consolidated and annotated statutes in a variety of subject areas.

common law. Law made by judges of the Common Law courts in instances when their judgments give legal force to the customs and usages of the common people.

controlled vocabulary. A dictionary of descriptor terms, index terms, or identifier terms assigned by an editorial staff for use in identifying the subject matter of records in a database to solve some of the recall and precision problems in full-text and bibliographic databases. The records in a database might use terms in inconsistent ways. By using terms from the controlled vocabulary in search statements, records in which those terms otherwise would not appear can be recalled. By limiting a search to the descriptor field or requiring a term to appear in the descriptor field, a search can be narrowed and false hits reduced or eliminated.

***Corpus Juris Secundum* (CJS).** A legal encyclopedia published by West Publishing Company that covers American law on a national scale.

***Current Law Index* (CLI).** An index to legal periodicals from U.S. and Commonwealth jurisdictions published by The Gale Group, formerly Information Access Corp. This index covers more periodical literature than the *Index to Legal Periodicals* but began later, in 1980. See "*Legal Resource Index*" and "LegalTrac."

Crown Copyright. In Canada, the government's claim of copyright, even in relation to its own citizens, in information it produces, such as court opinions.

Decennial Digest. A unit of the American Digest System. Each *Decennial Digest* covers opinions for ten-year periods starting in 1897. Prior to the *Ninth Decennial Digest*, all of the *Decennial Digests* were issued in one part only, covering the entire ten years. Now they are issued in two parts. See "American Digest System."

Dialog. A commercial online database service providing access to hundreds of databases of bibliographic, directory and full-text information. Materials include text of articles from hundreds of newspapers, magazines, newsletters, trade journals, newswires, and encyclopedias, indices to articles in medical periodicals, abstracts from psychological and sociological journals, corporate information, and patent and trademark information.

digest. The term "digest" may refer either to a one-paragraph summary of points decided in reported opinions of the courts, or to a set of books containing such summaries organized by subject matter. Regarding the latter sense of the term, see "American Digest System."

(legal) encyclopedia. Commentaries that attempt to cover most areas of the law very broadly in an arrangement of subjects similar to general encyclopedias. The major encyclopedias are *American Jurisprudence Second Edition* (Am.Jur.2d) and *Corpus Juris Secundum* (CJS).

factum. In Canadian practice, the written argument put before an appellate level court.

Federal Register. A daily publication of the federal government containing new, adopted, and proposed administrative regulations; executive orders and other executive documents; and news from federal agencies such as announcements calling for applications for federal grants. Many of the adopted regulations are later codified in the *Code of Federal Regulations*. See "*Code of Federal Regulations*" and "code, codify, codification."

FolioViews. A full-text search and retrieval program used extensively for CD-ROM and Internet legal research databases.

Grateful Med. A software package for searching MEDLINE, TOXLINE, CANCERLIT, HEALTH, AIDSLINE, and other National Library of Medicine (NLM) databases. Grateful Med includes a full-text document-ordering module called Loansome Doc.

headnote. A one-paragraph summary of a portion of a court opinion. The group of headnotes for an opinion is printed just before the beginning of the opinion. In West's reporters, all headnotes are numbered consecutively and the corresponding numbers appear in brackets inserted into the text of the opinion to aid in finding the portion of the opinion from which the headnote was digested. In West's reporters, each headnote also is assigned a topic and a number in the West Key Number system, and is later printed in West's digests. See "American Digest System."

hornbook. A law school text explaining the basic principles of a particular subject of the law. See also "textbook."

HTML. Hypertext Markup Language. The coding scheme used for designing and displaying documents on the Web.

Index to Legal Periodicals. An index to hundreds of legal periodicals from U.S. and Commonwealth jurisdictions. Available in print, CD-ROM and online versions on Westlaw and Lexis.

InstaCite. An online case citator available on Westlaw. See "citator."

intranet. A proprietary, organization-specific network that uses software programs based on the Internet TCP/IP protocol and common Internet user interfaces such as the Web browser.

Key Numbers. See "West Key Number system."

KeyCite. An online case citator proprietary to Westlaw. See "citator."

KWIC (Key Word In Context). A display format that shows portions of a document containing one or more of the search terms used in a query. The terms, whether single words, phrases or numbers, are highlighted and surrounded by twenty-five words on either side in the Lexis service and fifteen words in the MEDIS, Nexis, Lexis Financial Information and NAARS services. See also VAR KWIC.

law review. A legal periodical or journal of scholarly commentary on the law typically published and edited by law school students with contributions from students, faculty and legal scholars. Some law reviews are published by bar associations and private companies and tend to be more practice-oriented.

Legal Resource Index. The same material as in the *Current Law Index* provided on microfilm, LegalTrac, CD-ROM, Westlaw, and Lexis.

LegalTrac. A CD-ROM version of *Legal Resource Index.*

legislative history. Information about a statute as it passed through the various stages of the legislative process, from proposal through committee consideration, floor debate, conference, amendment, and signature by the executive. Various legislative bodies keep different amounts of information on the history of their enactments. Courts consult legislative history to determine the purpose and intent of the legislature when construing or applying a statute.

LEGI-SLATE. An online service provided by a wholly owned subsidiary of The Washington Post Company, that covers federal legislation, regulations, news and analysis. Its Custom Services Division tracks legislation and regulations for all fifty of the United States.

Lexis-Nexis. A very large, commercial online information service covering law, general news, accounting, business, and financial news and information. The Lexis service provides primarily American, English, European, and international legal material. American materials include: federal and state statutes and court opinions; Code of Federal Regulations; administrative decisions; Martindale-Hubbell Law Directory; ALR annotations; special libraries on taxation, insurance, and international law; treatises published by Commerce Clearing House and the Bureau of National Affairs; citators; and public records. The Nexis service provides the full text of articles from hundreds of news sources including newspapers, newsletters, magazines, and wire services. Additional services cover accounting, patents, medicine, and other information.

loose-leaf service. A print publication with removable pages that subscribers can update. The content can range from reprints of cases, statutes, or regulations within a specialty, to added features such as summaries and practice suggestions. Some loose-leaf services are comprehensive within a specialty. Some provide material not available elsewhere in print.

Maritime Law Books. A family of Canadian case reporters that use a topic-number classification system, including *British Columbia Appeal Cases, Alberta Reports, Saskatchewan Reports, Manitoba Reports, National Reporter, Federal Trial Reports, Atlantic Provinces Reports, Western Appeal Cases, Ontario Appeal Cases, Yukon Reports, New Brunswick Reports, Nova Scotia Reports, and Newfoundland and Prince Edward Island Reports.*

Martindale-Hubbell. A multi-volume directory of lawyers. The set also gives short summaries of the law of the fifty United States and many foreign countries.

Medline. The bibliographic database of the U.S. National Library of Medicine and a primary source for information from the biomedical literature. It is the computerized counterpart of *Index Medicus*, and also contains citations that appear in the Index to Dental Literature and the International Nursing Index. Medline contains references to articles from more than 3200 journals in all languages starting in 1966.

natural language. Natural language searching allows a search engine to process a query stated in a natural language, such as English, without the need for the searcher to learn an artificial search language syntax.

noting up. In Canadian practice, checking the current status and validity of a case by examining its history and references to it in subsequent decisions, typically through the use of citators. See "citators."

(West) Nutshell Series. A West Publishing Company series of more than seventy softbound, single-volume textbooks written by authorities on topics ranging from accounting and finance to workers' compensation and employment protection laws

OCLC. Online Computer Library Center, Inc. is a nonprofit, membership organization whose network and services link more than 30,000 libraries in sixty five countries and territories. OCLC helps libraries locate, acquire, catalog, access, and lend materials. Among its services are: WorldCat (the OCLC Online Union Catalog), the world's largest and most comprehensive bibliographic database; OCLC FirstSearch, an online reference service that provides flexible searching and subject access to more than seventy databases for end users; and OCLC FirstSearch Electronic Collections Online, which provides remote access to large collections of journals through the Web.

OPAC. Online public access catalog. The card catalog of a library accessible online.

opinion. A court's written statement of a case, its decision, and its reasoning leading to the decision. Terms often used interchangeably for "opinion" are "case" and "decision."

PREMISE. PREMISE Research Software is a product of the West Group that allows a researcher to access and search material stored on CD-ROM disks and magnetic media using natural language, fields templates or terms and connectors queries. It is designed for use with West CD-ROM Libraries and can also be used to access Westlaw.

primary authority. Statements of law by original sources. Depending upon the political theory underlying a legal system, primary authority can include constitutions, statutes, cases, court rules, administrative regulations, executive decisions, ordinances and treaties.

QuickCite. A proprietary case citator for Canadian cases on QuickLaw.

QuickLaw. An online legal information service providing material from Canada, Australia, and the United Kingdom. The service includes Canadian statutes, comprehensive coverage of full text Canadian cases since 1986, a Canadian case citator, a variety of Canadian case digests and topical reporters, Australian cases, and some United Kingdom cases.

regulations. In American law, see "administrative regulations." In Canadian law, regulations are subordinate legislation passed by the provincial or federal Cabinet pursuant to delegated powers in Acts of the legislature or parliament.

relevancy ranking. Arranging a set of retrieved records so that those most likely to be relevant to a request are shown first based on a measurement of similarity between the query and the content of each record. Different ranking algorithms consider a wide variety of measurements and assign differing weights to those measurements. Examples of the measurements are: breadth of match (the more query terms appear in a document, the higher the weight of relevance); inverse document frequency (terms rare within the entire database receive a higher weight of relevance); frequency (the number of times a query term occurs in a document); density (the comparable length of retrieved documents); term proximity (how close to each other search terms are in a record); term placement (where in a record the search terms appear, e.g., title, descriptor field, etc.).

reporter, reports. A series of books that report the full text of court opinions. An official reporter is published under the full authority of the government and typically includes the decisions of a single court. An unofficial reporter is printed by private companies, such as West, without special authority from the government. An unofficial reporter might cover a single court or the courts within a stated geographical region.

RLIN (Research Libraries Information Network). An international bibliographic database provided by the Research Libraries Group. The database contains electronic cataloging records for the holdings of materials owned by the top research institutions of the United States as well as some international institutions. RLIN includes information for books, serials, theses, dissertations, maps, and non-print materials.

secondary authority. Statements of law by sources other than original sources to which the courts give weight. Secondary authority includes treatises, textbooks, legal periodicals, legal encyclopedias, hornbooks, law dictionaries, and ALR annotations. These sources essentially comment upon the law by means of analysis, synthesis, description, explanation, restatement, and reorganization.

Shepard's, Shepardize. Citators published by Shepard's McGraw-Hill. See "citators." The term "Shepardize" means to use a citator to check on the subsequent history and current validity of a case. While "Shepardize" is used generically, it is actually a registered trademark of Shepard's McGraw-Hill.

SilverPlatter. SilverPlatter Information Retrieval System (SPIRS) search software for Windows, DOS, Macintosh, UNIX, and the Web produced by SilverPlatter Information Srl. The software is widely used for CD-ROM databases.

star paging, star pagination. Notations inserted into the text of a court opinion in an unofficial reporter indicating where the page breaks are in the official report of the opinion. When quoting from a case, these notations allow a researcher to cite the page within the opinion being quoted according to its pagination in the official reporter, even when a copy of the official reporter is unavailable. The notations are often flagged by a star, asterisk, or other symbol, hence "star pagination."

statute. A legislative enactment of law.

statutes at large. An uncodified, more or less chronological, printing of statutes. See "code, codify, codificaton."

Supreme Court of Canada Reports Service. Indexed digests of Supreme Court of Canada decisions since the formation of the Court. Published by Butterworths.

syllabus. A summary of a court opinion printed before the opinion itself. In a few official reporters, the syllabus itself is official and may even be written by the court. Most often, however, editors write the syllabus to aid research and it is not an official statement of the law.

synopsis. A summary of a court opinion.

textbook. A single-volume treatise on some topic of law in textbook form intended primarily for teaching law. Some textbooks are so highly regarded that they also have value as secondary authority. In the law, for historical reasons, a textbook is often called a "hornbook."

thesaurus. To build a set of search terms (term expansion), a searcher might use, among other things, any of three types of thesauri: general thesauri (e.g., *The New Roget's Thesaurus of the English Language in Dictionary Form*), specialized subject thesauri (e.g., *Thesaurus of Engineering and Scientific Terms*); or the hierarchical thesaurus of an online file. A hierarchical thesaurus might exist in printed or online versions, or both. See "controlled vocabulary."

treatise. A book or set of books that provide an extensive treatment of a topic of law, often including commentary, analysis, opinion, and recommendations for improvement or harmonization of various points within the topic.

***United States Code* (USC), *United States Code Annotated* (USCA), *United States Code Service* (USCS).** The *United States Code* is an annotated codification of the federal statutes of the United States. See "code, codify, codification" and "annotated code." The *United States Code* is published by the U. S. Government Printing Office. Two private publishing companies provide alternate and competing annotations. The *United States Code Annotated* is published by West Publishing Company and the *United States Code Service* is published by Lawyers Cooperative Publishing Company.

***United States Code Congressional and Administrative News* (USCCAN).** A set of semimonthly paperback supplements published by West Publishing Co., with annual bound volumes for each session of Congress, which provides, in Statutes at Large order, the full text of all public laws, with page references to where selected legislative history materials appear in the set. USCCAN prints the full text of those congressional committee reports most useful for legislative history research, references to other committee reports, and debates on the floor of Congress, and also (since 1986) statements made by the president when signing a bill. Finding aids include tables showing where new public law sections are classified in the USC and where USC sections are amended by new public laws, legislative history tables arranged by public law number, enactments arranged by bill number, popular name tables, and a subject index.

URL (Uniform Resource Locator). The address of a Web page or other Internet resource.

VAR KWIC. A display format that shows portions of a document that contain one or more of the search terms used in a query. The words, whether they be single words, phrases, or numbers, are highlighted and surrounded by a default of fifty words on either side in the Lexis service and thirty words in the MEDIS, Nexis, Lexis Financial Information, and NAARS services. The VAR KWIC format also lets a searcher determine the number of words in the display from 1 to 999. See also KWIC.

West Digest. See "American Digest System."

West Key Number system. A "Dewey Decimal system" for law; a subject classification system for legal subject matter created by West Publishing Company for use in its case reporters, case digests, and citators, to facilitate legal research. See "American Digest System" and "headnote."

Westlaw. A very large, commercial, online, full-text legal information service provided by West Publishing Company. Databases include federal and state court opinions, United States Code, state statutes, Code of Federal Regulations, administrative decisions, treatises published by West, Commerce Clearing House, Bureau of National Affairs, Prentice-Hall, legal periodicals, a directory of lawyers, federal topical libraries (securities, antitrust, labor, patents and trademarks, and more), state topical libraries (corporations, insurance, securities, and more), and non-legal data from other services such as Dow Jones and Dialog.

XML (Extensible Markup Language). A standard that allows Web site developers to extend HTML by creating their own tags and interpreters for those tags.

Index

C

P

Q

U

V

W

X

Y

Z

About the Author

T.R. Halvorson is a practicing attorney, legal researcher, author, computer programmer, and small grains farmer. He is licensed to practice before the U.S. Supreme Court, the Eighth and Ninth Circuits of the U.S. Court of Appeals, and the courts of Montana. He obtained his B.S.B.A in accounting and economics from the University of North Dakota and his J.D. from the University of Montana School of Law, where he was on the staff of the Montana Law Review. He has authored *How to Avoid Liability. The Information Professional's Guide to Negligence and Warranty Risks* and *Legal Liability Problems in Cyberspace: Craters in the Information Highway*, as well as articles in *Searcher*, *Law Library Resource Xchange*, and *EContent* (formerly *Database*).

T.R. is a member of Beta Alpha Psi, various bar associations, and the Association of Independent Information Professionals. He is an Eagle Scout, Pro Deo et Patria (American Lutheran Church), Ordeal Member of the Order of the Arrow, and past Outstanding President and Lt. Governor of Kiwanis International.

He lives with his wife, Marilyn, and their three sons on the breaks overlooking the Yellowstone River, known to Native Americans as the Elk River, just upstream from its confluence with the Missouri. He may be reached at pastel@lyrea.com or through his web site at www.netins.net/showcase/trhalvorson.

About the Editor

Reva Basch, executive editor of the Super Searchers series, is a writer, researcher, and consultant to the online industry. She is the author of the original Super Searcher books, *Secrets of the Super Searchers* and *Secrets of the Super Net Searchers*, as well as *Researching Online For Dummies* and *Electronic Information Delivery: Ensuring Quality and Value*. She writes the Reva's (W)rap column for *ONLINE* magazine, has contributed numerous articles and columns to professional journals and the popular press, and has keynoted at conferences in Europe, Scandinavia, Australia, Canada, and the U.S.

A past president of the Association of Independent Information Professionals, she has a Master's in Library Science from the University of California at Berkeley, and more than 20 years of experience in database and Internet research. Reva was Vice President and Director of Research at Information on Demand and has been president of her own company, Aubergine Information Services, since 1986.

She lives with her husband and three cats on the Northern California coast.

About the Author

About the Editor

NET.PEOPLE
The Personalities and Passions Behind the Web Sites
Thomas E. Bleier and Eric C. Steinert

With the explosive growth of the Internet, people from all walks of life are bringing their dreams and schemes to life as Web sites. In *net.people*, authors Bleier and Steinert take you up close and personal with the creators of 35 of the world's most intriguing online ventures. For the first time, these entrepreneurs and visionaries share their personal stories and hard-won secrets of Webmastering. You'll learn how each of them launched a home page, increased site traffic, geared up for e-commerce, found financing, dealt with failure and success, built new relationships—and discovered that a Web site had changed their life forever.

Available: Feb. 2000 • Softbound • ISBN 0-910965-37-4 • $19.95

UNCLE SAM'S K-12 WEB
Government Internet Resources for Educators, Students, and Parents
Laurie Andriot

Uncle Sam's K-12 Web is the only comprehensive print reference to federal government Web sites of educational interest. Three major sections provide easy access for students, parents, and teachers. Annotated entries include site name, URL, description of site content, and target grade level for student sites. *Uncle Sam's K-12 Web* helps children safely surf the Web while enjoying the many fun and educational Web sites Uncle Sam offers—and guides parents and teachers to the vast amount of government educational material available online. As a reader bonus, regularly updated information and links are provided on the author's Web site, fedweb.com.

1999 • Softbound • ISBN 0-910965-32-3 • $24.95

INTERNET BLUE PAGES
The Guide to Federal Government Web Sites
Laurie Andriot

With over 900 Web addresses, this guide is designed to help you find any agency easily. Arranged in accordance with the US Government Manual, each entry includes the name of the agency, the Web address (URL), a brief description of the agency, and links to the agency or subagency's home page. For helpful cross-referencing, an alphabetical agency listing and a comprehensive index for subject searching are also included. Regularly updated information and links are provided on the author's Web site.

1999 • Softbound • ISBN 0-910965-29-3 • $34.95

Electronic Styles
A Handbook for Citing Electronic Information
Xia Li and Nancy Crane

The second edition of the best-selling guide to referencing electronic information and citing the complete range of electronic formats includes text-based information, electronic journals and discussion lists, Web sites, CD-ROM and multimedia products, and commercial online documents.

Softbound • ISBN 1-57387-027-7 • $19.99

Net Curriculum
An Educator's Guide to Using the Internet
Linda C. Joseph

Linda Joseph, popular columnist for *MultiMedia Schools* magazine, puts her K-12 and Internet know-how to work in this must-have book for teachers and school media specialists. This is a practical guide that provides dozens of exciting project ideas, plus information on accessing information, electronic publishing, building Web pages, researching online, copyright and fair use, student safety, and much more.

Softbound • ISBN 0-910965-30-7 • $29.95

The Modem Reference, 4th Edition
The Complete Guide to PC Communications
Michael A. Banks

> "If you can't find the answer to a telecommunications problem here, there probably isn't an answer."
> —Lawrence Blasko, *The Associated Press*

Now in its 4th edition, this popular handbook explains the concepts behind computer data, data encoding, and transmission; providing practical advice for PC users who want to get the most from their online operations. In his uniquely readable style, author and techno-guru Mike Banks (*The Internet Unplugged)* takes readers on a tour of PC data communications technology, explaining how modems, fax machines, computer networks, and the Internet work. He provides an in-depth look at how data is communicated between computers all around the world, demystifying the terminology, hardware, and software. *The Modem Reference* is a must-read for students, professional online users, and all computer users who want to maximize their PC fax and data communications capability.

Available: Mar. 2000 • Softbound • ISBN 0-910965-36-6 • $29.95